SAVING
DINNER
BASICS

SAVING DINNER BASICS

**How to Cook Even If
You Don't Know How**

LEANNE ELY

BALLANTINE BOOKS · NEW YORK

A Ballantine Books Trade Paperback Original

Copyright © 2006 by Leanne Ely

Published in the United States by Ballantine Books, an imprint of The Random House Publishing Group, a division of Random House, Inc., New York.

BALLANTINE and colophon are registered trademarks of Random House, Inc.

Illustrations by Sandy Strunk

Library of Congress Cataloging-in-Publication Data
Ely, Leanne.
  Saving dinner basics: how to cook even if you don't know how / by Leanne Ely.
    p. cm.
  ISBN 0-345-48543-2 (pbk.)
  1. Cookery. I. Title.
TX651.E47 2006
641.5—dc22   2006045962

Printed in the United States of America

www.ballantinebooks.com

9 8 7 6 5 4 3 2 1

Text design by Helene Berinsky

This book is lovingly dedicated to my darling Dan,
whose steadfast love and devotion have become
a pillar in my life. I love you with my whole heart.

ACKNOWLEDGMENTS

This time around, I have to start my acknowledgments with my extraordinarily long-suffering editor, Caroline Sutton. To say she has the patience of Job wouldn't begin to speak of her endurance. Caroline, I appreciate you beyond measure—you're a gem!

Once again, my wonderful agent Michelle Tessler has done a fabulous job, crossing all the t's and dotting all the i's. Attention to detail is what makes Michelle the stellar agent that she is!

I dedicated this book to Dan, but I need to mention Dan again. It's a joy to live with you, sleep with you, eat with you, and love you. You are indeed the love of my life and now the whole world knows it, too.

In addition to my children, Caroline and Peter, who have suffered through each book I've written, Meredith—my new daughter—has learned how much fun it is when Mom's writing a book (said tongue in cheek). You guys are the best—thanks for your patience.

My wonderful assistant Kandi Speegle continues to thrive in her unpredictable (yet exhilarating, right, Kandi?) job and still hasn't complained (so far). She keeps me fueled with triple venti cappuccinos (skim milk, slightly dry) and tells me (subtly, sorta) when it's time to get the highlights in my hair "refreshed." This woman has been there and done it all, and has somehow managed to do it with a smile on her face. Thank you, Kandi, for *all* you do!

Bonnie Schroader is the genius behind our website, including the newly designed gorgeous eye-candy of a site, www.savingdinner.com. If you haven't been there in a while, you owe it to yourself to get over there and go for a stroll. Her hard work and constant creativity have made our site what it is, not to mention the hundred other things she does in a given day. A huge thank-you to you, Bonnie, for everything!

Marla Cilley (yes, *the* FlyLady) is everything her cartoon character is and then some. Having a true friend like Marla in my life is one of the biggest blessings I've ever experienced. Thanks, Marla; you've been there for me, in good times and bad—I'm forever appreciative.

The SavingDinner.com team continues to do an awesome job, and to each of them—Nikki, Sherri, Cathy, Robyn our bookkeeper, and the rest of the customer service staff—a great big, hearty thank-you!

CONTENTS

PART TWO: **RECIPE READY**

INTRODUCTION

Home Ec, that once-ubiquitous high school class where cooking and sewing reigned supreme, has left the building. The school building, that is. They don't teach it anymore, as far as I can tell. At least, based on the e-mails I receive here at Saving Dinner Central. Perhaps today's Home Ec (if it does exist) has more to do with putting takeout restaurants on speed-dial than actually cooking something. Cooking has become somewhat of a lost art, and I feel it is my duty to help people of all ages and stages of life to reclaim it.

I have had a lot of e-mail over the years asking for help with basic cooking skills. I have explained to my various correspondents in excruciating detail how to chop an onion (and how to safely wield a knife on a variety of other vegetables that need processing); how to tell when pasta is done; how to cook a butternut squash; how to sauté or simmer; and how to determine when something has reached a "rolling boil." I have explained in laborious specifics which foods to freeze and which not to freeze; how to measure (dry and wet ingredients alike); and how to purée in batches, as opposed to all at once and having the soup explode all over the kitchen (including the ceiling), giving new meaning to the term Rorschach test. One of my all-time, perplexing e-mails came from a Menu-Mailer subscriber who claimed that it took her an hour to prepare a simple recipe—with a full five minutes to chop *one* lowly onion! That's when I knew: these folks need some real help with the basics.

This book will explain that the kitchen is more than a room with large appliances in it. And that the kitchen is actually the heart of the home, where you can make good smells emanate at meal-appointed times, just as your mom did. Cooking isn't brain surgery; it isn't even as complicated as removing a tricky splinter. With the simple explanations in this step-by-step, get-you-through-it guide, *Saving Dinner Basics* will help you get beyond the intimidation factor and cook with full confidence.

The goal of *Saving Dinner Basics* is to be a quick go-to guide to what's important in the kitchen, and what you need to know to cook with my cookbooks at least. The other stuff not included in this book? Well, there are tons of huge, comprehensive tomes out there that promise to teach you to do everything else in a kitchen that you may or may not want to do. As for me and my house, we'll stick with what's on these pages, thank you very much. Life is easier when you're not wringing your hands over a puff pastry recipe.

What sets *Saving Dinner Basics* apart from your mother's basic cookbook is that it's fun, it's hip, and it's simple without all the fuss. The other day I was reading in a "basic cookbook" about how to mince garlic. It was a three-step process, complete with pictures. To that I say, *fuggedaboutit!* What a colossal waste of time. Get a garlic press and get on with it, already. Why spend 3 minutes of your life on a 5-second task for the same result? That's how *Saving Dinner Basics* is different—we're going to have some fun here and toss out the stuff that doesn't matter.

A Note from My Editor

Caroline Sutton, my very proficient editor (and very capable home cook) at Ballantine, made some great points when we were discussing this book. What stayed with me in particular was when she said, "I'm a good cook because I don't think there is a right way and a wrong way. There is a way that works and a way that doesn't. The one that works is the one that produces results that I like and therefore want to eat."

I like that. So true! We tend to get hung up on this notion that we have to "do it right" or not at all. Caroline takes this concept a step further and says, "Julia Child might be grading my mother, but she is not grading me. Nor is she eating my dinner."

Isn't that a relief? To know that it isn't about being "perfect" in the kitchen? It really is time to get over ourselves and get on with it. A few techniques and some know-how under your belt, and you too can give the directions the boot (as my editor would) and improvise on ingredients. For right now, though, let's get you over the kitchen's threshold. You gotta start somewhere; and from where I stand, that would be right where you are. Let's get busy!

WHO NEEDS THIS BOOK?

David Letterman is famous for his nightly top-ten lists. It's been a long time since I stayed up late enough to catch Letterman, but I have been known to create a top-ten list myself on occasion. So . . . may I have a drumroll, please?

THE TOP TEN REASONS YOU MIGHT NEED THIS BOOK
(in descending order of importance):

10. You think you know how to cook because you know the difference between the microwave and the DVD player.
 9. You think a wok is something you take your dog on.
 8. You think folding egg whites has something to do with laundry.
 7. You had to take out a second mortgage on your house to finance your takeout habit.
 6. Your idea of a happy meal is when your mom does the cooking.
 5. The only reservations you have about cooking are in the yellow pages under "Restaurants."
 4. The contents of your refrigerator's crisper resemble a 6th-grade science fair project on slime.
 3. When your smoke alarm goes off, the kids ask, "What's for dinner?"
 2. The local drive-thru sends you a Christmas card every year.
 1. The neighbors are beginning to think you have a "thing" for the pizza guy!

PART ONE

BASIC KNOW-HOW

CHAPTER ONE

EQUIPPING THE KITCHEN: TOOLS OF THE TRADE

It seems like the world is obsessed with the gizmos and gadgets that illustrate a cutting-edge kitchen, rather than interested in the more utilitarian (and admittedly less snazzy) kitchen that gets plenty of use. I remember years ago when I was catering that one of my clients had this amazing kitchen—a six-burner Wolf range, a fabulous Sub-Zero fridge, and all the latest and greatest tools a person could lust for. And yet, this poor woman would have to call her mother to figure out how to boil a pot of water. She was totally hopeless in the kitchen. She looked great, her kitchen looked great, but the bottom line? She was a wannabe cook and couldn't find her way around that kitchen, even with an illustrated map.

Most people don't want to live out their culinary lives with kitchen "sets"—they really want to cook and make things happen in the kitchen, like breakfast, lunch, and dinner and an occasional dessert, too. To get there, you're going to need to make sure your kitchen is ready for real-life action, and not a photo shoot for a magazine. That means you are going to need tools and equipment, not gizmos and gadgets—there's a big difference.

So let's get to it, shall we? Get your kitchen tricked out with what you need, and leave the junk behind. I have lots of suggestions here: equipment and such that is essential, and a good description of how to set up your own kitchen. Once you're really cooking (preferably with gas), then you can add some more goodies to your basic setup. You'll figure out what you want to add as you go along—that's how your kitchen reflects your own unique cooking personality. Maybe you've taken pasta making to a new level; it is completely appropriate for you to buy a pasta machine so you can make your own. This is what I mean by having kitchen tools and appliances that reflect your own unique cooking style. Just be careful! I've never met a kitchen store I didn't find irresistible. It's easy to fall madly in love with an expensive gadget and promise yourself that you will soon be making homemade ice cream or pasta. Inexpensive gadgets are much easier to justify (hey, it's only five bucks), but these one-trick items can crowd your drawers and cupboards and make the essential necessary tools hard to find when you need them. Being discerning has saved me from chucking expensive (and inexpensive) nonessential equipment to the Goodwill.

If cooking is something you are still reticent about, let me appeal to your inner nurturer. Cooking is a soul-satisfying activity. Cooking a meal provides food and nurturing to those you love most in the world. Providing food and sustenance for your family (and doing it in a tasty and fun way) is a gratifying daily job that is more a joy than a drudgery—if you have the eyes to look at it that way. It starts with having the right tools, getting your pantry stocked, and then actually doing something in the kitchen with those tools and foods.

Cooking with Gas, Literally

If you are fortunate enough to have a choice of what you'll be cooking on (gas or electric), you'll definitely want gas. Gas gives you better control of the heat; a gas stove heats almost instantaneously, cools down quickly, and is the first choice of professional chefs. Electric stovetops seem to do the exact opposite and frustrate pros and novices alike.

But what do you do if you're stuck with electric? Here are some tips for coping:

1. Make sure the burner elements are working properly. They sometimes need replacing, so make sure yours are in top working mode.

2. Match the size of the pan to the element. Not only is it wasteful energy-wise to put an 8-inch pan on a 10-inch burner, but it also could produce a scorching result, not to mention the chance of burning yourself.

3. Keep the burners clean. When an electric stovetop is clean, it reflects the heat better and saves energy as well.

4. Flat-bottomed pans are the key to even cooking. The element must have full contact with the pan in order to produce decent results.

5. Turn the heat off way before the cooking time indicates, especially if you need to take it down from a rolling boil to a simmer. This will help you simmer your food without burning, because electric coils take longer to cool down than gas flames.

I want to start this section with a letter I received from a perplexed reader asking for some direction and help in setting up her kitchen. This letter will help you get a good visual on how to set up your own kitchen:

Dear Dinner Diva,

I have a new apartment and don't know exactly how to set up my kitchen—where do I put everything? Where should everything go? I have plenty of below- and above-cupboard space—and a few drawers. I have a big stash of vitamins, too, that I don't know what to do with.

I've gotten rid of my fast-food habit by cooking at home (and make my own fast-food by chopping everything up in advance so all I have to do is put it together when I want something to eat), but the kitchen isn't efficient. Do you have any ideas on how I can do this?

Thanks in advance for any help,

Distraught in Detroit

Dear Distraught,

First off, I want to commend you for getting your act together by getting rid of the fast-food habit. Your "assembly-line" approach to doing your own, homemade fast food is an inspiration, good for you! One word of caution is not to get too far ahead. By day four, your stuff is going to start looking pretty rank. You want to chop and store just enough for a couple of days, ideally.

You asked a great question that bewilders many a newbie with a first kitchen: where does everything go? On one hand, that's difficult to say without seeing your kitchen; but on the other hand, there are some logical ways to discuss this without ever having to see it. You mentioned that you have plenty of below- and above-cupboard space. So let's start there and see what we can do.

I like to put like with like. In other words, keep the baking stuff together, the pots and pans together, and the utensils together. Seems real basic, but you can't imagine some of the kitchens I have worked in. They just didn't make sense.

If you have a small bank of drawers, put your silverware in a plastic silverware tray with the different compartments for each utensil (very cheap at a discount store), and put that in the top drawer. You may want another plastic utility tray in the same drawer (if it will fit) for holding your serving utensils.

You can buy these plastic trays in two sizes—narrow or wide. They help keep things sorted rather than your having to dig through a drawer— really smart for keeping you from getting cut, too, because knives should never be thrown into a drawer without being contained and controlled in some fashion (in my opinion). This is what I've done with all my kitchen drawers. Use another drawer for other miscellaneous utensils like a potato peeler, a grater, can opener, etc. Again, use utility trays if you can.

I use another drawer for plastic wrap, foil (heavy-duty for roasting and regular), plastic bags (zipper type, all sizes, and freezer and regular weights), waxed paper, parchment paper (great for those who bake and those who don't—parchment is a multitasking paper), and my rolling pin, believe it or not. Great place for it. I also have a drawer for just my towels and dishrags. I buy them in bulk from a restaurant-supply store, so I have white muslin towels and bar rags like you see in restaurants. They wear very well; when they are ugly I use them as rags, and when they wear out I dump them.

Choose a cupboard for your food pantry (unless, of course, you have a proper pantry). I put the canned stuff all on one shelf and again: like goes with like. If you have four cans of tuna, place them all together. Stack them even. Don't have them scattered throughout the cupboard or you won't know where anything is, especially when you need it. I do the same with dried goods, keeping the pastas together, as well as rice, oatmeal, and cereals. I also use small plastic baskets for envelopes of spice blends, bags of dried beans, and other miscellaneous and sundry items needing a place to live in my pantry that wouldn't do well sitting by their lonesome on a shelf.

On the bottom shelf of my pantry, I keep a bin for onions and another one for potatoes and sweet potatoes. Are you seeing the pattern? It makes good sense because all things are complementary to one another.

When it comes to the actual dishes and serving pieces, keep in mind that your dishware should be close to the silverware for easy table setting. I keep my mugs and glasses in one cupboard right above the coffeemaker: glasses on one shelf, mugs on another. Everyone knows that if you need something to hold a drink, you go to that particular cupboard. When I make my coffee in the morning, the cups are right where they should be— on the first shelf in the cupboard above the coffeemaker. The whole ebb and flow of the kitchen is to have it make sense. When it is set up that way, it will be easier to work in when you need to grab something in the middle of cooking or serving.

You mentioned that you have a lot of vitamins. So do I. The way I handle keeping them from being all over the place is to place them all together in a large basket. I use baskets for everything. They contain everything beautifully, and when it's time to take your vitamins, you just pull the basket (or baskets) out, get your vitamins, put them back in the basket, and voilà! Easy as pie!

In my old house, I had my spices in a spice rack that I hung on the wall right above the stove. That is one option for anyone who likes the convenience of having spices handy while cooking (however, they will age a lot faster by being right above the heat). In my new house, I use a drawer and cupboard right next to the stove. Either one works—it just depends on your setup. The spices I keep in a drawer are the little half-size jars. On each lid top, I mark what it is with a Sharpie (abbreviated, of course). That way, when I need to grab a spice in a hurry when I'm cooking, I don't have to stop and try to figure out which one I need. I keep frequently used cooking utensils on the stovetop (like big spoons, wooden spoons, spatulas, wire whisks, etc.) in a big crock. I find it helpful and easy to get something I need right away.

That's it in a nutshell. I sincerely hope that helped!

Best wishes,

The Dinner Diva

YOUR BASIC BASIC KITCHEN

Now that you understand where to put things, you need to know what to get so you can put them where they need to go. Did you get all that? Well, never mind, then. Just keep reading. . . .

KNIVES

Sharp, high-quality knives are first on the list. This is one place you cannot afford to skimp. Buy a good brand (I've used Henckels for more than 20 years now) and you'll have them for your entire cooking career.

First up on the list is a basic cutting and chopping knife. A 6- to 8-inch **chef knife** (or the same-sized **santoku knife**, which is a Japanese knife used for the same chopping abilities) is the ticket. Don't be intimidated by this large a knife. Once you learn how to hold it and chop with it (don't worry, I will teach you how!), you won't believe you could ever cook without one!

Next is the **paring knife**. Again, we're talking quality here—no cheapie, 99-cent plastic-handled number you picked up at the dollar store. In a pinch, on your way to a picnic, maybe—but you can't use a knife like that every day in the kitchen or, I promise, you will end up hating to cook. Quality tools *do* make a major difference. Paring knives have smaller blades, 2½ to 3 inches long. This is the knife you will use to peel or pare an apple and trim the ends off radishes or Brussels sprouts.

Serrated knives will help you slice a tomato like a pro, cut bread into slices, and cut up citrus with ease. The toothy blade makes all the difference. My preference is a larger and a smaller serrated knife (one of each)—the larger knife for bread, the smaller one for the citrus and tomato slicing.

You can't have Thanksgiving (or any other holiday requiring a slicing up of the holiday fowl or beast) without a large **carving knife** and fork. The blade on these knives is typically long and flexible, enabling you to negotiate corners and carve neatly. If you can, purchase the carving knife and fork set together. I have the same lovely set I received as a gift more than 20 years ago, and they work just as wonderfully now as they did all those years ago when I struggled to carve my first Thanksgiving turkey.

Two other knives you probably *won't* need are a **boning knife** and a **filleting knife**. And guess what you'll do with these knives? Bone and fillet! Now, let me tell you how often I use my boning and filleting knives. About once a year, if that. The bottom line is, if I need something boned or filleted, I have my butcher take care of it for me. Why? Is it because I don't know how to do it or because I'm lazy? The answer is yes to both. I can painstakingly bone a chicken breast or another piece of meat, and I can fillet, too. But not well. This is why we ask the butcher to do it. This is what he does for a living and you don't. Besides, you have other things to do besides boning and filleting poultry or other meat, don't you? I'm glad we discussed this. So for the sake of having a full set of knives, make sure you have your boning and filleting knives. We'll all sleep better at night knowing you have a complete set.

Blade Runner

If you notice your knives beginning to dull (and they will naturally from use), you will want to sharpen them. One thing I don't recommend is buying anything that has you consigning your blades to a "knife sharpener." Don't do it. Your knives will suffer and you will regret it. These sharpeners, no matter how tricked out or expensive, can't offer the same control you can. You need only two things to get your knives in shape.

The first one is a **steel.** Generally, this will come with your knife set (if you bought it that way); otherwise you will need to buy one. It's long, has a handle, and looks like a sword—somewhat. Mine has a little ring attached to the handle so that it can be hung up for easy use in the kitchen. If you're a professional, hanging up your steel is always an option—mine stays put in the wood block it came in.

Anyway, to sharpen a knife you need to hold the knife with the hand you would normally cut with. In the opposing hand, you will want to grip your steel, upright like a flagpole. Holding the knife at a 25-degree angle (or thereabouts), move the blade down one side of the steel, making sure to get the whole knife moving. Now do the other side of the knife. You can do this a few times, but make sure to do both sides evenly. I always count when I do mine.

Using a steel is more of a maintenance thing than a sharpening thing, really. If your blades are in dire need of a good sharpening, you'd be wise to take them to get professionally sharpened. Ask for a referral at a quality kitchenware shop or see if this is a service it offers. You can also check the phone book or check on-line for somewhere close by where you can get your blades handled, but make sure you get them sharpened professionally at least once a year.

So now you're asking me how to use that santoku or French knife—the big one. Okay, believe it or not, this is easy. First you will need to use both hands—one for holding whatever it is that you're cutting (that will be the opposite hand you will be cutting with) and the other to cut with. The hand that holds the food we will temporarily transform into a claw. Yes, a claw. Why a claw? Glad you asked. Because when you are holding the food in a clawlike fashion, if your knife accidentally gets too close to your fingers, the worst that will happen is that your fingers will get too close a shave, but you won't be losing any digits to the santoku!

Now, as far as making the chopping go smoothly and quickly like they do on Food TV, well, that just requires a rhythm, which will come as you get better at chopping. The idea is to "rock" the blade slightly as you chop. This will build a rhythm and eventually your speed. Next time you're watching the Food Network, pay attention as Emeril chops effortlessly. He's got his claw going; he's a-rockin' and a-choppin'—the whole thing is an art form. Remember, though, that you're not Emeril. Go easy and slow, and be careful. These are sharp knives we're working with here, not rubber spatulas.

After you have your knives in order, there are few more objects to get your basic kitchen stocked—some stuff you'll already have, some stuff you wouldn't have thought about:

- *Several cutting boards.* Working with just one cutting board is a mistake. With all the scary information out there on salmonella and the rest of the creepy germs that can sneak into your food, it might not be a bad idea to be a little more kosher about your cutting boards: use one for vegetables, fruit, etc., and one *only* for meat, poultry, and fish. It's a lot cleaner. You can buy these hard plastic cutting boards in various sizes (and colors so you can color-code—green is for veggies, blue is for meat, etc.) for next to nothing at discount stores. They wear out, too, you know, and the cutting lines you carve into your boards can harbor all kinds of icky bacteria. You will want to replace them as they start getting a little "hairy" in the cutting area.

- A *flat-bottomed wok*. This is a tool I have owned for a very long time. This stainless, well-seasoned pan has cooked more stir-frys than a Chinese takeout. This wonderful pan can cook for two or do veggies for a whole crowd. I truly wouldn't be without it. The flat bottom is an essential feature to the wok—no fussing with a ring and a wobbly pan on the stove. It makes a huge difference in whether you will love or hate this particular pan and whether or not it will be used often. Having a flat bottom may not fit well in a pair of jeans, but for a wok, a flat bottom is a perfect fit.

- *Vegetable steamer*. Unless you forget about your vegetables in the steamer and steam the daylights out of them, you almost can't wreck them. The vegetable steamer helps to save the nutrients in the veggies, too, rather than have them boil out into the water. The steamer is a little stainless-steel number that blooms open like a flower when you're using it and then retracts to a nice little round bun-looking thing when you're not using it. It's a great, inexpensive tool that belongs in every kitchen.

- *Stainless or nonaluminum cookware*. Aluminum has been linked to all kinds of health problems, and rather than debate the issue, why not just get some decent stainless-steel pots and pans and forget about it? My faves are the Calphalon stainless-steel ones (Calphalon skillets I especially like), but there are other brands to be had. I bought a terrific set (Italian-made) at Costco that had all the aforementioned criteria—top-grade stainless-steel pots and pans with heavy bottoms so the food doesn't burn easily, well-built handles (plus a secondary handle on the other side of the larger pans for easy handling), and pots and pans that clean up easily (no odd nooks and crannies or weird angles—you can tell by the basic construction if it will clean up well). Make sure, too, that the entire pan is made of stainless-steel—no goofy plastic handles that will melt if your recipe calls for sticking the skillet under the broiler to melt some cheese or something. The deal is to not get hung up on name brands but to look for the clues to real quality. I have no idea who made my pots and pans, but it's a private label and I bet it is a top-notch manufacturer.

  What about nonstick coated pans, you ask? Well, read on and

you'll find out that I do own one. I think a set of nonstick cookware is a mistake; however, a nonstick skillet is pretty much essential.

- A *stash of 9 × 13–inch baking dishes*. You can fill and throw these in your freezer. If you can get in the habit of doubling your family's dinner, you can stock a mother lode of meals in the freezer with very little extra effort. I am partial to the Pyrex brand because of the durability factor. In fact, I've been a Pyrex fan for years and years, and occasionally I need to buy more—not because they're broken or worn out, but because I bring something in them to a party and forget where I left the dish!

- A *timer!* If you are like me, your good intentions can turn into burnt offerings. A good working timer with a buzzer or a bell you can actually hear in the laundry room with the washer and dryer going full speed ahead is really smart. Why go to all the trouble of cooking if you can't get the lasagna out of the oven before it's Italian history? Trust me, you *need* a timer!

- *Wire whisks*. Make sure they are quality wire whisks, too, not the cheapie kind. I have three in various sizes: a huge balloon whisk for the big jobs, a medium one (this one does most of the work around here), and a smallish one for the little jobs, like eggs or a quick sauce. I also have a plastic-coated whisk that I use in my large nonstick Calphalon skillet. There is nothing better than a good whisk for making scrambled eggs (or prepping eggs for a recipe), making sauces, gravies, etc. A wire whisk is an unbeatable, necessary, have-to-have tool. Keep several on hand.

- *A good stash of wooden spoons*. My friend Sharon brought me back a wooden spoon from France that I am just in love with. The engineering of the spoon is perfect for stirring anything, and it just feels good in my hand. I have only one in my crock of stirring implements, but it's the first one I grab if it's not dirty. My goal is to get more of those lovely spoons in different sizes.

- *Kitchen linens*. As for me and my house, we use stuff from the restaurant-supply store. I'm not kidding. I loathe the matchy-matchy stuff from department stores. I especially hate oven mitts and consider them nearly useless. I do use one little handwoven one that my daughter made me when she was eight years old, but other than that, I use clean terry towels or white muslin towels the way they do in professional kitchens. You learn how to use them to pick stuff up in a hurry—trust me on that one. If you insist on using oven mitts, get some that are thick enough on the bottom but flexible on the top so you don't feel like your arms are stuck in a robotic stance.

- *Microwave*, but only for quick heatups, like melted butter or zapping a leftover. I am still not sold on this idea of microwave cooking. Yeah, I know microwaves have come a long way, baby. But in my book, it's still just an appliance for helping you cook, not for doing the actual cooking. It's not that it's cheating, necessarily (and believe me, I cheat and take shortcuts all day long with my cooking), but it's that they cook weirdly. I'm not convinced that rearranging the food's molecules through zapping is the best way to cook.

- *Pizza stone*. (Good-bye, pizza parlors!) You will be sold on how wonderful this thing is. I use mine for heating rolls and making garlic bread, too. A girlfriend of mine uses hers for cookies as well.

- *Kitchen scissors*. You can cut up chickens easily, snip herbs, cut dough for cinnamon rolls—you can even stick your scissors into a can of gloppy tomatoes (although that kind of grosses me out, to be honest) and snip away to get chopped tomatoes. Truly an indispensable tool and, again, something you can pick up at a discount store. I have had expensive kitchen scissors and cheap ones, and although the expensive ones are little nicer, for what you're using them for the inexpensive ones are just fine. (Buy a second pair and stash them for emergencies. I guarantee a child will abscond with the primary pair at some point.)

- *Dry measuring scoops*. I recommend at least two sets. You can get very nice stainless-steel scoop sets at discount stores. I put a 1-cup measuring cup in my flour canister and a ½-cup measuring cup in my sugar canister. My brown sugar canister has a ¼-cup measuring cup in it. True, I often need a different measurement, but sometimes it's just the amount I need; if it's not, the other set of measuring cups is sitting in a drawer, ready for action. This works well and it's one less thing to think about when you're trying to measure something for a recipe. Always use the back of a knife to scrape off the top for an accurate measure. When measuring flour, you will want to spoon it into your measuring cup, and then use the knife to scrape off the top. If you scoop the flour using the measuring cup, you might measure a tad too much and wreck your recipe.

- *A good supply of zipper-type bags.* All sizes and the freezer kind, too. Yes, they are worth the extra money—your freezer stuff will really hold up better. They're great for marinades, storing doughs, soups, a big ol' meat loaf, frozen veggies (once you've opened the original bag), and a whole host of other foodstuffs, too. One must-have tool is a Sharpie pen. Hide it in the plastic wrap so no one walks off with it. Then you can even mark the contents and date on your bags! What a concept—to actually *know* what's in your freezer and how old it is! How completely organized can you get?

- *A good stash of plastic storage containers.* Not everything fits well in a zipper-type bag, so those little plastic storage containers are just the trick. I buy the "disposable" ones at the grocery store rather than invest hard-earned money in ones that need to be hand-washed (as if!) and cost a day's wage to own. Not only that, but when you consider how often you need to purge your plastic container storage drawer (or cupboard) because of the mismatches (tops and bottoms), you would be wise to take my advice—especially if they are on sale and you have a coupon!

CHAPTER TWO

A PANTRY PRIMER

In this day and age, a pantry is more than a mere closet in which to store dry goods and canned items. When I think pantry, I think about the fridge and freezer, too. After all, this large item also does a good job keeping food handy. Shelf life isn't as long, but it's an important tool for the cooking and making of meals.

Before you can properly stock a pantry, you need to destock it and make sure it's ready to hold the stuff you want in there. This goes for the fridge and freezer, too.

You know what I'm talking about when I say you have to destock first. Just like a bookshelf can be bursting with books, making the contents nearly unusable, so can a pantry be bulging with so much stuff that it turns your most important dinner- (and other meal-) producing asset into a landfill. I am going to bet you have stuff sitting on those shelves that you will never eat in a million years. There are probably boxes of half-eaten cereal, bought on sale (with a coupon) that the kids gave the big thumbs-down to, and they've been sitting there taking up precious space for well over six months: canned veggies missing the label, the old dented cans in the back of the cupboard, and the hearts of palm or other gourmet goodies that you have no idea why you bought it in the first place. There could be expired stuff hanging out in your pantry, too. This stuff must go! Anything decent and still edible can be taken to a food bank, but the rest must simply go in the trash. If you do this one simple exercise, you will experience the thrill of getting your pantry logically arranged and ready to work for you. Don't brush this off—this has to be the starting place. For me, my neat and spiffy pantry brings a sense of calm because I can navigate through my cooking duties knowing what is (and what isn't) there.

Here's how this works: grab a trash bag and a sturdy cardboard box—you will use the bag for the trash and the box for the food bank. Organize your pantry by putting like items together: all your baking supplies together in one spot, all your canned goods, all your cereals—you get the picture. When grouping the canned goods, you will want to put the tomato products together, the chicken broth, etc., together—not just toss the canned stuff all together or you won't be able to accurately inventory what you have. Soon the pleasure of a pleasing pantry will begin to emerge. You will be able to make sense out of the thing, and before you know it, the end result of your labor will be a Perpetual Pantry that will dispense what you need when you need it.

Your own Perpetual Pantry must reflect what is consumed in your home. Our family doesn't eat canned soups; consequently there is no canned soup in my pantry. You may eat canned soups (and that's fine!), so you need to include what you eat in your pantry. I know that is a big "duh," but I've had so many e-mails from people asking me what they need in their pantries. That's almost a trick question, and because I'm not clairvoyant, I've yet to answer it accurately and to the inquiring individual's liking. Is it any wonder? I do have a basic pantry list (and I've included it here), but you will need to customize it to fit your family's parameters. That's how you get your own pantry going.

Besides grouping like with like (as mentioned above with regard to canned goods), you'll also want to keep the shelves divided into categories of food. Put the cereals and grains (rice, pasta, oatmeal, dried beans, etc.) together on one shelf or in one area. Place baking stuff together on another shelf. The object is to organize it so it makes sense to you. Think grocery-store layout on a small scale. The same goes for the freezer: put all the meats together, juices together in the door, veggies, ice cream, etc., and next thing you know, you'll be able to *find* stuff!

That doesn't mean you have to be a perfectionist and start lining stuff up in alphabetical order! Being the proud owner of a Perpetual Pantry doesn't need to be a full-time job. It does mean that you'll spend a little time in your cupboard and in your freezer, but this can be done while you're on the phone with a friend or are helping a child, who's sitting at the kitchen table, with homework—just a little at a time when you have a spare moment. You want to be able to smile every time you open your pantry doors because it's neat and organized, and you know that what you have in there works for your family. Your Perpetual Pantry is the key to kitchen organization and food prep.

You've seen the bumper sticker, "He who dies with the most toys wins." Well, for a pantry, this is a bad idea. This is not the goal at all; the goal is to get the food you need in there so it will *serve* you and your family. Your well-stocked pantry doesn't mean crammed to the gills so that you need to post a sign that says "Beware of falling objects."

I have included below a basic list of things you're going to want in your pantry, especially if you'll be cooking some of the recipes in this book and in my other *Saving Dinner* books. The second part of this pantry equation is to keep the food easy to find (as mentioned above) and also to rotate your foods so your older stuff gets used first.

Remember: your pantry doesn't have to be the equivalent of a scavenger hunt—it needs to be a place where you can get what you need to make what you want.

- *Canned items and jarred items.* All manner of **tomato products:** diced tomatoes, whole tomatoes, spaghetti sauces, pizza sauce, tomato paste, salsas. I keep a variety of sizes available, too. **Canned beans:** black beans, pinto beans, kidney beans, garbanzo beans, whatever bean you can find that you'll eat. It's less expensive to use dried beans, but canned are still cheap and will work in a pinch. I'm also fond of already canned baked beans and bean dips. You can doctor them with a little bacon and some brown sugar, and they taste like homemade. **Canned seafood:** tuna, salmon, crab, clams. **Canned fruit and vegetables:** stock the ones you like and will use. I have pineapple, applesauce, mandarin oranges, pears, peaches, whole cranberries, cranberry sauce, pumpkin, corn, olives, roasted red peppers, jars of tapenade, mushrooms, artichoke hearts, pesto (tomato and basil), canned chilies, tomatillos, anchovies, capers. **Canned soups and broths:** stock the ones you use. I use a lot of chicken broth (low-sodium has more flavor), beef broth, vegetable broth, and bottled clam juice; enchilada sauces (green and red), jars of gravy (great for extending what you made). **Canned milk:** sweetened condensed and evaporated—both work great in baking.

- *Condiments.* Ketchup, mustards (yellow, Dijon, whole-grain), pickles (dill and sweet), relish, mayonnaise, A-1, Worcestershire sauce, Tabasco, stir-fry sauces, soy sauce (low-sodium, if you can find it), teriyaki sauce, horseradish sauce, cocktail sauce. Once opened, store in fridge (except soy sauce, unless labeled that it needs to go in the fridge).

- *Oils and vinegars.* Vegetable oils of choice (I like a cold-pressed safflower or sunflower oil by Hollywood), olive oil, sesame oil for stir-fry. All oil except olive oil will go rancid staying out and must be refrigerated after it is open. White and red wine vinegar, apple cider vinegar, and balsamic vinegars.

- *Nut butters and jelly.* Peanut butter (crunchy or creamy), almond and cashew butters, jelly, jam, fruit spread, conserve, honey. My peanut butter needs to be refrigerated after opening. Check your label to be sure.

- *Herbs and spices.* To keep the price down on these spices, go to a dollar store or Wal-Mart to stock up as much as possible. You can also go to a health food store and buy everything you need from the bulk jars. This is the best place to get quality spices and be frugal at the same time, believe it or not. I've bought the freshest spices at the health food store for 35 cents each. Basil, thyme, marjoram, rosemary, dill, garlic powder, onion powder, cayenne, red pepper flakes, cumin, chili powder, paprika, oregano, ginger, dried mustard, cinnamon, peppercorns for the peppermill, nutmeg, and curry powder are in my spice cabinet because I *use* all of them. I also use sea salt and kosher salt, and have both of those in my spice cabinet. Buy only what you use.

- *Baking center.* Sugar (white, brown, confectioners'), flour (white, whole wheat, other), cornmeal, pancake mix (I hope you make mine—see page 73), baking powder (should be kept in a cool dry place and don't forget to check the expiration date!), baking soda, salt, cornstarch, baking chocolate, cocoa, vanilla, chocolate chips, nuts, baking mixes (corn bread, cake, brownie, etc.).

- *Pasta, rice, and grains*. An assortment of pastas that you will use. Lasagna noodles, spaghetti noodles, ziti, rotini, fusilli, fettuccine, linguini—only what you use. Boxed macaroni and cheese (try the natural white cheddar kinds. They are really good—got a great recipe using them in here, too). Rice—I much prefer brown, but get what you'll use. I've also got basmati rice, wild rice, and some blends and mixes. Oats, split peas, dried beans (white beans, navy beans, black beans, pinto beans), lentils, barley, couscous.

- *Breads and cereals*. Whatever you use. Bread should go in the freezer if it doesn't get used right away. Tortillas should be stored in the fridge—I prefer whole wheat (without trans fats) tortillas for burritos and corn tortillas for tacos and fajitas.

- *Potatoes, squash, and onions*. Russets, Red Rose potatoes, sweet potatoes, butternut squash (or other whole squash in season, except summer squashes, which need refrigeration), brown and/or yellow onions, red onions. Keep potatoes away from the light or they turn green. Also, don't store potatoes next to apples. Apples give off a gas that causes potatoes to sprout.

- *Miscellaneous pantry items*. Coffee, assorted teas, hot cocoa, etc.

PANTRY MEALS

These recipes are absolute lifesavers when you're crunched for time and have no imagination left. I can't tell you how many times one of these babies has saved my reputation!

My Freezer, My Friend

Where would I be without my faithful companion, my freezer? Inside of its chilly little body are the fixin's for meals, desserts for good boys and girls, and on occasion, some ice for a boo-boo. Freezers are one of those appliances that have made my life easy and bargain hunting doable. Crock-Pots (slow-cookers) are another, but that's another chapter! Every time the market has a "buy one, get one" sale on something worthwhile, where does it go? The freezer—because the freezer is our friend.

I would be remiss not to mention that the freezer can also hold an already prepared dinner or two; the beauty of a chilly dinner is the ease of accomplishment—a definite boon to busy working moms. Next time you're making something your family loves, double or even triple the recipe and freeze the bounty. Double freezer-bag it for long-term storage and mark the contents and date with a Sharpie pen—the only brand of pen with ink that won't run. I keep the pen in the box of zipper-type bags to avoid it being absconded by roving bands of children. There is almost no extra work in making three meat loaves vs. one—all you need are the ingredients. And the nifty thing is, if you pull out the meat loaf to thaw in the fridge in the morning before you go to work, it'll be a quick warm-up in the evening when you get home. By the time the potatoes are done and the salad is tossed, you'll have a delicious dinner ready to roll.

Sometimes we're caught way off guard and need a meal in a hurry. Having your pantry to rely on is an awesome way to relieve stress, believe it or not. Knowing what's for dinner is half the battle in getting dinner on the table. And on those days when your day went south after your first cup of coffee, it's nice to know you can pull a rabbit out of your hat at the last minute. At least dinner doesn't have to be a disaster! Here are some terrific recipes that will help you pull this off. Most ingredients in these recipes are things you pull out of the pantry or freezer.

LINGUINI WITH CLAM SAUCE

Serves 4–6

1 pound linguini (uncooked)
3 (6-ounce) cans minced clams, with liquid
1 (14.5-ounce) can low-sodium chicken broth
¼ cup (½ stick) butter
2 garlic cloves, pressed
2 tablespoons flour
½ cup clam juice
⅛ teaspoon dried thyme
Dash of Tabasco
¼ cup chopped fresh parsley
1 tablespoon lemon juice
Salt and pepper

Prepare pasta according to package directions. Drain.

While pasta is cooking, drain the juice from the canned clams into 2-cup measure, then add enough chicken broth to make 2 cups liquid.

In skillet, melt butter over medium-high heat and sauté the garlic. Stir in flour. Cook on low for about 1 minute, stirring constantly.

Gradually stir in clam–chicken broth liquid, clam juice, thyme, and Tabasco. Bring to a boil and simmer 1 to 2 minutes.

Stir in clams, parsley, and lemon juice and heat through. Add salt and pepper to taste. Serve over hot linguini.

PER SERVING:
497 Calories; 11g Fat; 32g Protein; 66g Carbohydrate; 2g Dietary Fiber; 78mg Cholesterol; 282mg Sodium. Exchanges: 4 Grain (Starch); 3 Lean Meat; 0 Vegetable; 0 Fruit; 1 1/2 Fat; 1/2 Other Carbohydrates.

GARLIC CORN CHOWDER

Serves 4–6

3 garlic cloves, pressed
3 tablespoons butter
1 medium onion, chopped
1 green bell pepper, de-ribbed, seeded, and chopped
3 cups diced potatoes, peeled
2 cups low-sodium chicken broth
1 (16-ounce) can cream-style corn
1 (8-ounce) can corn kernels, drained
1 (16.5-ounce) can evaporated skim milk
Salt and pepper

In a skillet over medium-high heat, sauté garlic in butter until garlic is fragrant. Be careful not to burn garlic. Add onion and bell pepper, and continue to sauté until onion is translucent, about 4 minutes.

Add potatoes and broth; simmer until potatoes are tender, 15 to 20 minutes.

Stir in corn and evaporated milk. If soup is too thick, add up to 1 cup water. Season to taste with salt and pepper.

PER SERVING:
230 Calories; 1g Fat; 14g Protein; 46g Carbohydrate; 3g Dietary Fiber; 3mg Cholesterol; 564mg Sodium. Exchanges: 2 Grain (Starch); 1/2 Lean Meat; 1/2 Vegetable; 1/2 Nonfat Milk.

IMPOSSIBLY STUFFED FRENCH TOAST

Serves 6

12 slices raisin bread
8 ounces cream cheese, softened
All-fruit strawberry spread or jam
12 eggs, beaten
4 tablespoons vanilla extract
Vegetable oil
Confectioners' sugar
Real maple syrup

On 6 slices of bread, spread a layer of cream cheese. On the other 6 slices of bread, spread a layer of strawberry jam. Place 1 slice of cream cheese bread together with 1 slice strawberry jam bread to form a sandwich. Repeat with remaining slices until you have 6 sandwiches.

In a large bowl, mix eggs and vanilla. Carefully dip each sandwich into the egg batter.

In a skillet, heat a little vegetable oil (about 1 teaspoon or so) over medium-high heat. When pan is hot, add 3 sandwiches and cook till the egg is cooked through and the toast is golden brown. Flip and cook just as on first side. Remove and keep warm. Repeat with remaining sandwiches.

Serve warm with a little confectioners' sugar sprinkled on top and maple syrup.

PER SERVING:
581 Calories; 30g Fat; 22g Protein; 61g Carbohydrate; 8g Dietary Fiber; 415mg Cholesterol; 761mg Sodium. Exchanges: 3 Grain (Starch); 2 Lean Meat; 1/2 Fruit; 5 Fat; 0 Other Carbohydrates.

TACO PIZZA CASSEROLE

1 (8.5-ounce) package corn muffin mix
1 egg
3 tablespoons milk
½ cup chopped onion
1 tablespoon vegetable oil
1 (15-ounce) can chili, no beans
1 (15-ounce) can diced tomatoes with chilies, drained
½ teaspoon red pepper flakes, or to taste
1 cup shredded low-fat cheddar cheese
Salsa (your favorite jarred variety)
Low-fat sour cream

Preheat oven to 400°F.

Mix corn muffin mix, egg, and milk according to package directions. Spread in bottom of lightly greased 9 × 13–inch casserole dish.

In a skillet over medium heat, sauté onion in oil. Add chili and diced tomatoes, and heat until warm. Spoon chili mixture onto corn muffin mix. Sprinkle with red pepper flakes and cheese.

Bake for 15 to 20 minutes, or until crust is cooked through and cheese is melted and lightly browned on top.

Garnish with salsa and sour cream as desired.

PER SERVING:
310 Calories; 13g Fat; 9g Protein; 42g Carbohydrate; 7g Dietary Fiber; 45mg Cholesterol; 865mg Sodium. Exchanges: 1/2 Grain (Starch); 1/2 Lean Meat; 1 Vegetable; 0 Nonfat Milk; 2 Fat; 2 Other Carbohydrates.

WHITE BEAN AND CHICKEN FUSILLI

Serves 4–6

12 ounces fusilli (uncooked)

2 garlic cloves, pressed

1 tablespoon olive oil

*2 (10-ounce) cans chunk white-meat chicken, drained, or 3 cups
  chopped cooked chicken breasts*

1 (15.5-ounce) can white beans, drained

2 (14.5-ounce) cans diced tomatoes

1 tablespoon Italian seasoning

Grated Romano cheese

Prepare pasta according to package directions. Drain.

While pasta is cooking, sauté garlic in oil over medium-high heat for a couple of minutes. Add chicken, beans, tomatoes, and Italian seasoning. Bring to a low boil, decrease heat, and simmer sauce for 10 minutes to let flavors blend. Stir frequently.

Divide pasta among plates and serve sauce on top. Garnish with Romano cheese.

PER SERVING:
517 Calories; 12g Fat; 36g Protein; 66g Carbohydrate; 6g Dietary Fiber; 62mg Cholesterol; 538mg Sodium. Exchanges: 4 Grain (Starch); 3 1/2 Lean Meat; 1 1/2 Vegetable; 1 Fat.

ROASTED PEPPER AND BLACK BEAN SOUP

Serves 4–6

1½ (14.5-ounce) cans diced tomatoes
1–2 cups water
½ teaspoon chili powder, or to taste
1 (15.5-ounce) can black beans, drained
1 (9-ounce) jar roasted red peppers in water, drained and chopped
Baked tortilla chips
Sour cream
Salsa (your choice)
Shredded low-fat cheddar cheese

Combine tomatoes, 1 cup water, chili powder, and black beans in a large saucepan or stockpot. Bring to a low boil over medium-high heat.

Remove about 2 cups from saucepan and place in blender or food processor. Purée till smooth and return to saucepan.

Add roasted red peppers and stir to incorporate. If soup is too thick, add up to 1 cup water. Bring to a boil, reduce heat, and simmer for about 10 minutes.

Ladle soup into bowls. Garnish with tortilla chips, sour cream, salsa, and cheese as desired.

PER SERVING:
422 Calories; 5g Fat; 15g Protein; 80g Carbohydrate; 12g Dietary Fiber; 3mg Cholesterol; 729mg Sodium. Exchanges: 5 Grain (Starch); 1/2 Lean Meat; 1 1/2 Vegetable; 0 Nonfat Milk; 1 Fat.

Serves 4–6

Corn tortillas

2 (10-ounce) cans chunk white-meat chicken, drained, or 3 cups
    chopped cooked chicken breasts

½ cup water

½ (1.25-ounce) package low-sodium taco seasoning

1 (16-ounce) can fat-free refried beans

1 cup chunky-style salsa (your favorite)

1 cup shredded low-fat cheddar cheese

Chopped fresh cilantro

Preheat broiler.

Toast tortillas lightly in broiler just long enough for them to become slightly crisp. Watch them like a hawk—you don't want them to become so crisp that they turn into tortilla chips. Set aside.

Place chicken in a large skillet over medium-low heat. Break chicken chunks apart, if needed. Add water and sprinkle with taco seasoning. Stir chicken to coat with seasoning and continue to stir until most of the water is evaporated from chicken. Be careful not to scorch.

Warm refried beans in saucepan over low heat, stirring occasionally. Once beans are warm and smooth, remove from heat.

Spread a layer of refried beans on top of each tortilla. Top each tortilla with chicken, salsa, and cheese. Place tortillas on baking sheet and return to broiler. Broil for just a minute or so, until cheese is melted.

Garnish with chopped cilantro and serve.

PER SERVING:
329 Calories; 10g Fat; 31g Protein; 27g Carbohydrate; 6g Dietary Fiber; 63mg Cholesterol; 1326mg Sodium. Exchanges: 1 1/2 Grain (Starch); 4 Lean Meat; 1/2 Vegetable; 0 Fat; 0 Other Carbohydrates.

QUESADILLAS (PANTRY-DILLAS)

Serves 4–6

2 (10-ounce) cans chunk white-meat chicken, drained, or 3 cups
  chopped cooked chicken breasts
½ cup water
½ (1.25-ounce) low-sodium taco seasoning
Burrito-size flour tortillas (I prefer whole wheat)
1 cup shredded Monterey Jack cheese
½ cup sour cream
½ cup guacamole

Preheat oven to 425°F.

Place chicken in a large skillet over medium-low heat. Break chicken chunks apart, if needed. Add water and sprinkle with taco seasoning. Stir chicken to coat with seasoning and continue to stir until most of the water is evaporated from chicken. Be careful not to scorch.

Place about ½ cup of chicken on one side of each tortilla. Top with cheese, a dollop of sour cream, and a dollop of guacamole. Fold the empty side of the tortilla over the filling and place tortilla on baking sheet.

Bake for about 10 minutes or until cheese is melted and quesadillas are warmed through.

Cut each quesadilla into wedges and serve with sour cream and guacamole.

PER SERVING:
540 Calories; 25g Fat; 33g Protein; 44g Carbohydrate; 3g Dietary Fiber; 84mg Cholesterol; 1150mg Sodium. Exchanges: 2 1/2 Grain (Starch); 3 1/2 Lean Meat; 0 Nonfat Milk; 3 Fat; 0 Other Carbohydrates.

JUST LIKE THANKSGIVING CASSEROLE

Serves 4–6

¼ cup bread crumbs
½ teaspoon dried thyme
½ teaspoon dried sage
4–6 turkey cutlets
Salt and pepper
1½ tablespoons olive oil
1 cup low-sodium chicken broth
⅓ cup cranberry sauce
⅓ cup orange marmalade

Combine bread crumbs, thyme, and sage in a shallow pie plate or 8-inch-square baking dish.

Dredge turkey cutlets in bread crumb coating and season with salt and pepper to taste.

In large skillet over medium heat, sauté turkey cutlets in olive oil on both sides until turkey is cooked through, about 4 minutes each side. Remove turkey from skillet and keep warm.

Add broth to skillet and scrape the browned bits off bottom of skillet. Add cranberry sauce and marmalade. Lower heat and let sauce simmer a bit, stirring often till thickened.

Serve turkey cutlets with sauce.

PER SERVING:
473 Calories; 20g Fat; 52g Protein; 20g Carbohydrate; 1g Dietary Fiber; 147mg Cholesterol; 272mg Sodium. Exchanges: 0 Grain (Starch); 7 Lean Meat; 1/2 Fat; 1 Other Carbohydrates.

Serves 4–6

4–6 boneless skinless chicken breast halves
2 tablespoons olive oil
1½ tablespoons chopped fresh basil
Salt and pepper to taste
2 (14.5-ounce) cans diced tomatoes (undrained)
1 (9-ounce) jar roasted red peppers in water, drained and chopped
1 tablespoon capers, rinsed and drained

In large skillet over medium heat, sauté chicken in olive oil until firm. Season with basil, salt, and pepper. Brown chicken on both sides for about 5 minutes, but don't worry about cooking it through. Once chicken is browned, remove from pan.

Add tomatoes to skillet and scrape browned bits off bottom of pan. Add peppers and capers to skillet, then return chicken to skillet. Reduce heat, cover, and simmer about 10 minutes or until chicken is cooked through.

Serve chicken topped with sauce from pan.

PER SERVING:
213 Calories; 7g Fat; 29g Protein; 10g Carbohydrate; 3g Dietary Fiber; 68mg Cholesterol; 103mg Sodium. Exchanges: 0 Grain (Starch); 4 Lean Meat; 2 Vegetable; 1 Fat; 0 Other Carbohydrates.

GREEK ISLE CHICKEN

Serves 4–6

4–6 boneless skinless chicken breast halves
2 tablespoons olive oil
Salt and pepper
½ (6-ounce) jar Kalamata olives, drained and chopped
1 cup diced tomatoes (if canned, drain)
⅓ cup crumbled feta cheese
2 teaspoons Greek seasoning

Season chicken with salt and pepper to taste. In large skillet over medium heat, place chicken in oil. Brown chicken on both sides till chicken is cooked through, about 8 minutes per side, depending on thickness.

While chicken is cooking, prepare topping by combining olives, tomatoes, cheese, and seasoning.

Place chicken on serving plates. Top with olive, tomato, cheese, and seasoning mixture and serve.

PER SERVING:
234 Calories; 11g Fat; 29g Protein; 3g Carbohydrate; trace Dietary Fiber; 75mg Cholesterol; 389mg Sodium. Exchanges: 0 Grain (Starch); 4 Lean Meat; 0 Vegetable; 0 Fruit; 2 Fat.

CURRY IN A HURRY SHRIMP

Serves 4–6

1 (16-ounce) package sauce-free frozen oriental vegetables
1 tablespoon olive oil
3 (6-ounce) cans tiny shrimp
1 (14-ounce) can coconut milk
1 tablespoon curry paste, mild or hot
⅓ cup dry-roasted peanuts

In large skillet over medium heat, sauté vegetables in olive oil for 2 to 3 minutes. Add shrimp and continue to cook for another 2 to 3 minutes.

Add coconut milk and curry paste. Stir to incorporate. Simmer for about 10 minutes.

Divide vegetables among plates, garnish with peanuts, and serve.

PER SERVING:
244 Calories; 12g Fat; 24g Protein; 9g Carbohydrate; 3g Dietary Fiber; 148mg Cholesterol; 259mg Sodium. Exchanges: 0 Grain (Starch); 3 Lean Meat; 1 Vegetable; 0 Fruit; 2 Fat.

SLAMMIN' SALMON WRAPS

Serves 4–6

1 (14.75-ounce) can salmon, drained and chunked

1 (8-ounce) package cream cheese, softened (I use light cream cheese)

3 green onions, minced

1 tablespoon lemon juice

2 teaspoons Italian seasoning

½ teaspoon onion powder

¼ cup salsa (your favorite jarred variety)

Burrito-size flour tortillas (I use whole wheat tortillas)

Romaine lettuce leaves

½ cup diced fresh tomato

½ cup shredded carrots (you can buy them already shredded)

1 cup thinly shredded cabbage (I use coleslaw mix)

1 cup broccoli slaw (comes in a bag in the produce section)

In a mixing bowl, combine salmon, cream cheese, green onions, lemon juice, Italian seasoning, onion powder, and salsa.

Spread salmon mixture onto tortillas. Top with lettuce leaves, tomato, carrots, cabbage, and broccoli slaw. Roll up, cut in half, and serve.

PER SERVING:
551 Calories; 18g Fat; 38g Protein; 66g Carbohydrate; 17g Dietary Fiber; 59mg Cholesterol; 1028mg Sodium. Exchanges: 2 1/2 Grain (Starch); 2 Lean Meat; 5 Vegetable; 0 Fruit; 2 Fat; 0 Other Carbohydrates.

CHAPTER THREE

HOW TO PICK PRODUCE, POULTRY, AND OTHER MEAT

Make no mistake about it: choosing your produce every week can be a little like courtship and marriage—you think you know who you're "dating," till you get him home and have to live with him. And just to make it even more difficult, the ever-increasing variety of what's available can be downright intimidating. Making the right choices produce-wise is confusing when you're just starting out. So what's a gal (or a guy) to do?

There are a number of solutions. Let's start basic and very easy, and build up. We'll do it in phases, okay? Deep breath; let's begin. Start with the work already done for you—that's a great place to push off. There is a bounty of fresh, available, and ready-to-go produce, all bagged up and just waiting to jump into your grocery cart. For simplicity's sake, let's call the ready-to-go stuff Phase One. We will go to Phase Two after mastering Phase One.

You don't need to know anything in Phase One: you just grab the bag (eyeball it first to make sure it looks good, then check for expiration dates), pay your money (yeah, this stuff isn't the cheapest way to go), and go home and use it. There are usually recipes on the bag, and I've got some ideas here, too, on how to use these convenient veggies.

With Phase One produce, it's easy to go recipe-less and build beautiful, nutrient-rich salads to suit just about everyone's palate. Just grab a bag and follow these great tips for quick and easy meals and side dishes.

- *Slaw.* You can go traditional and empty a bag of ready-to-go slaw into your salad bowl; add ½ of cup low-fat mayo, a teaspoon of honey, and a splash of cider vinegar, and you're ready to roll.

- *Ethnic slaw.* For fun, use a bag of broccoli slaw instead and add ½ cup low-fat mayo, a splash of rice wine vinegar, and a shot of sesame oil; then garnish with a little chopped cilantro and honey-roasted peanuts, and you're good to go.

- *Chips and dip.* Those great big carrot chips are a whole lot better for you than the potato kind! Open up a bag and serve with your favorite low-fat dip instead, and you'll save yourself a whole bag of calories!

- *Stir up.* For a quick and easy vegetarian stir-fry meal, chop some green onions and press a little garlic, then put it in a wok, already heated with a little oil. Add a bag of stir-fry vegetables, a dash of soy sauce, some ginger, and some bean sprouts, and you have a good meal. Put it on brown rice and you have a great meal!

- *Tofu tagalong.* There's tofu in the produce department. Maybe you'd like a few chunks of tofu in your stir-fry? Go ahead—don't be timid. Tofu can be fun.

- *Carrot slaw.* Much better than the kind your school cafeteria served. Mix a bag of shredded carrots with ½ cup low-fat mayo, a handful of raisins, and a generous pinch of chopped walnuts. Delicious!

- *My favorite salad.* In a large bowl, toss together from different bags whatever you have on hand (and I use a handful of the basic greens per person to make mine): field greens, baby spinach, shredded broccoli, shredded cabbages (smaller portions of the shredded stuff). Add thinly sliced green onion, a sprinkling of pine nuts, a generous portion of sun-dried tomato, and feta cheese crumbles. Toss together with a simple dressing of 1 pressed garlic clove and 2 parts rice wine vinegar to 1 part olive oil. Let sit for just a minute for flavors to meld (but not too long, otherwise your salad will be soggy). So good!

See how easy it is to buy produce? I know—it's kinda like cheating because it's already bagged and ready to go. But how about having to actually pick stuff out? Like a melon, perhaps? Buying a cantaloupe can be quite intimidating unless you know the tricks of the trade. This is Phase Three in the produce-procuring procedure and we will go there, but first let's hit Phase Two.

Choosing great produce isn't too difficult. The first easy hint is to eat in season. I've been a big advocate of eating in season for years for good reason—the price is right, the flavor is there (it is in season after all), and it just feels right. Eating watermelon in December somehow seems almost deviant, doesn't it? Likewise, why would you want a butternut squash in the middle of the summer? Turn on the oven and bake squash when it's 100 degrees outside? Not in my house! Summer fruits and vegetables are different from winter fruits and vegetables, and you need to differentiate so you buy the right stuff at the right time. Watch the sales and specials at your local grocery store, and you'll see what's in season (although there is quite a bit of produce coming from South America and Mexico now, so the seasons can get a little mixed up). Better yet, hit the local farmer's market to get a real picture of seasonal produce.

Once you've determined what produce you want to buy based on season (see chart), you'll want to start choosing your veggies. Believe it or not, for the most part, the veggies themselves will tell you what to get.

Seasonal Produce Chart

Vegetable	Fall Sep, Oct, Nov	Winter Dec, Jan, Feb	Spring Mar, Apr, May	Summer Jun, Jul, Aug
Apples	✓			
Apricots				✓
Asparagus			✓	
Avocados		✓	✓	
Basil			✓	✓
Beans			✓	✓

Vegetable	Fall Sep, Oct, Nov	Winter Dec, Jan, Feb	Spring Mar, Apr, May	Summer Jun, Jul, Aug
Beets			✓	✓
Berries			✓	✓
Broccoli	✓	✓	✓	
Brussels sprouts	✓	✓		
Cabbage	✓	✓	✓	
Cauliflower	✓	✓		
Cherries				✓
Chili peppers			✓	
Clementines		✓		
Corn				✓
Cranberries	✓			
Cucumbers	✓		✓	✓
Dates	✓			✓
Fennel	✓	✓		
Figs				✓
Grapes	✓			✓
Grapefruit		✓		
Greens	✓	✓		
Lettuce			✓	✓
Mangoes			✓	✓
Melons				✓
Mushrooms	✓			
Nuts	✓			
Okra	✓		✓	✓
Oranges		✓	✓	
Papayas			✓	
Peaches				✓
Pears	✓	✓		
Peas			✓	
Persimmons	✓			
Plums				✓
Pomegranates	✓			
Rhubarb			✓	
Shallots	✓		✓	
Spinach	✓	✓	✓	

Vegetable	Fall Sep, Oct, Nov	Winter Dec, Jan, Feb	Spring Mar, Apr, May	Summer Jun, Jul, Aug
Summer squash				✓
Sweet peppers			✓	✓
Sweet potatoes	✓	✓		
Tangerines		✓		
Tomatoes				✓
Turnips		✓		
Watermelon				✓
Winter squash	✓			
Zucchini				✓

You want stuff with no blemishes, flaws, or bruises. You want produce with good color, too. In other words, tomatoes should be bright red, not pink. Your green beans should have a deep green appearance, not a wimpy, celery-pale green. And there is always the sniff factor. You want your fruit to smell like the fruit it is supposed to be. If your peach smells like cardboard, chances are good it's not ripe and may have been picked too soon. You can administer the sniff test to any fruit or veggie with strong olfactory values. I'd skip sniffing the lettuce, however.

Organically Speaking

To go organic or not to go organic—that is a question that comes up over and over again. Increasing evidence suggests that what you think you are buying may not be all you are getting. They never list the pesticides, rodenticides, or herbicides your salad greens have been blasted with—yuck. Or the greasy wax on your apple—double yuck. Nor do they include information about genetic engineering, hormones, antibiotics, or irradiation. It might not be a bad idea to consider going organic.

I've spent the last 15 years of my life preaching healthful eating habits. I've spoken to small groups in schools and large groups in conferences. I've spoken to women, men, students, and anyone else who will listen. We absolutely need to bump up the quantity of fruits and vegetables in our diets if we're going to enjoy optimal health and remove the threat of obesity from our lives.

I've tread lightly on the organic issue (although I have been eating organically myself for years), but I am to the point now where I won't. Simply stated, organic is better. It tastes better, it's more nutritious (because it's picked at its peak, as opposed to when underripe), and it's becoming more readily available.

According to a June 1998 article in *Acres USA*, organic farmers have shown a higher nutrient content in their produce about 40 percent of the time, compared to conventional crops, which show a higher content only about 15 percent of the time. Data is based on more than 30 studies comparing nutrient content of organic and nonorganic produce involving more than 300 individual nutrients.

Yes, unfortunately organic is more expensive, and while I'm not trying to elicit guilt, it is my duty to tell you that not all fruits and vegetables are created equal. Try organic the next time you go to the grocery store and see what you think. You may become a convert yourself!

Once you've conquered Phase Two, you'll be ready to step up to Phase Three. Phase Three is for the more serious selectors of all things grown in the fruit and vegetable sector, or at least those shoppers who can choose a good tomato, feel good about their salad fixin's, and tell an asparagus from an avocado. If you've got all of the above conquered, you are definitely a Phase Three candidate—maybe even an advanced Phase Three consumer. What differentiates regular Phase Three folks from advanced Phase Three folks is melons. There are two kinds of people in life: those who pick good melons and those who do not.

We've all seen a good melon picker at the market or produce stand, circling the melons like an exotic bird beginning an elaborate mating dance. Then, when the moment is ripe, the melon picker swoops in and begins to thump, smell, and feel melons. But why all the fanfare and melon exhibitionism?

Because that is how you end up with a perfect melon. And to help you decode what exactly goes on in securing a good melon, here are some tips to unwrap forever the mystery of melons:

- *Go for the heavyweights.* The heavier the melon, the juicier it is. Pick up two same-size melons, and choose the heavier of the two.

- *Check the spot.* If the melon you are thinking of purchasing is a Persian, cantaloupe, or casaba, it will have a little indentation on the end where it was attached to the vine. The opposite end is the blossom end, and it is the blossom end that you should check for a little softness—not the indentation. A very common mistake with amateur melon pickers.

- *Nice complexion.* Certain melons, like honeydew and other smooth-skinned melons, have a light creamy yellow skin, not greenish blue. They should also have a velvety touch to them. Cantaloupes should look yellow under their netted skins, not green.

- *Sniff test.* A good melon will smell like a good melon. If you pick up a cantaloupe and can't smell it, chances are it was picked too early, and though it will soften up, the flavor will never be there.

- *Knock, knock.* Who's there? Watermelon. Watermelon who? A hollowish-sounding watermelon is a good pick. Ditto the yellowish underbelly of the dirigible-looking watermelon. Skip the watermelons with white undersides—they've been picked too soon. If the watermelon is cut, it should be firm, not mushy. The flesh should be beautifully colored and the smell potent.

- *In season.* Summer is definitely the time to buy melons. All of these tests will be much easier to administer to an unsuspecting melon if you're doing this midsummer, as opposed to Christmastime.

Once the produce has been picked and purchased, you're ready to hit the meat counter. So how do you go about determining the difference between good beef, bad beef, and so-so beef? And where *is* the beef, anyway? That was the cry heard 'round the world a few years ago by a little lady named Clara Peller, who got a tad upset when there wasn't enough ground round between her hamburger buns.

A lot has changed since then. Not only is it hip to beef up the protein in your meals, but today's poultry and other meats have become a lot leaner. One thing that has stayed the same is how to find the right cut and knowing what to look for. So let's mooove, ladies and gentlemen. Can I hear the drumsticks drumming, please? Here's a simple little list to make your trip to the meat counter a lot easier:

1. *Love me tender.* Make sure the meat you are purchasing is tender to the touch. If it is rough, that means the animal was either too old or stressed when it was butchered.

2. *Glean for lean*. There are lots of choices out there—make sure you look for the one piece that isn't too marbled. True, marbling means tender, but it also means *fat*.

3. *Old is gold*. Aged beef is better because the connective tissue breaks down, yielding a tenderer cut of beef. Look for beef that has been aged at least 14 days.

4. *In the thick of it*. A thicker pork chop is far superior to a thin one, unless you're a sucker for a good piece of shoe leather. Thick chops are more flavorful, much more tender, and much better eating.

5. *Sound ground round*. Check the labels of ground beef. Most supermarkets offer many different types of ground meat and give you the percentages of fat by weight right on the package. Look for the lowest percentage of fat to save big on calories and fat grams.

6. *Think pink*. Or red even, but never brown. Brown meat is a sign that it may be spoiled. Stay clear and go for the pink or red cuts of meat.

7. *The thigh's the limit*. When choosing poultry for your slow-cooker, dark meat is always best. Skinless boneless chicken thighs are an excellent choice as they are low in fat without the skin.

8. *Chilly chicken*. When buying poultry, make sure it is cold to the touch. A well-chilled chicken helps to prevent bacterial contamination. Keep your chick cool.

9. *The smell test*. Fresh poultry has a very mild scent, while unfresh poultry is rather pungent. Less is more in this olfactory exercise.

10. *Cook your goose*. Remember to cook poultry and other meats thoroughly. When you cut through to the center to test, the juices should run clear. Whole birds should register 180 degrees on the meat thermometer. You also need to know where to stick that meat thermometer. The thigh's the place, and make sure you don't touch the bone or you will get a false reading.

Here's a simple recipe for meat that will have you standing and cheering! Fire up the barbie and enjoy this easy recipe.

JAMAICAN JERK-STYLE STEAKS

Serves 6

6 (4–6 ounce) rib-eye steaks or other cut of your choice

DRY RUB

1½ tablespoons garlic powder

1½ tablespoons onion powder

3 tablespoons brown sugar

3 teaspoons salt

3 teaspoons dried thyme

3 teaspoons ground ginger

3 teaspoons ground allspice

1½ teaspoons black pepper

1½ teaspoons ground cinnamon

¾ teaspoon cayenne pepper

½ teaspoon ground nutmeg

Preheat barbecue grill. If you don't have a barbecue grill, plug in your George Foreman grill, pull out a stovetop grill pan, or turn on your oven broiler.

In a bowl, mix all the spices well.

Sprinkle the dry rub on one side of each steak, covering evenly. Rub the dry spice mixture into the meat. Flip the steaks over and repeat.

Grill over medium heat until steaks reach your desired level of doneness.

If broiling in oven, place meat about 5 inches from broiler and cook for about 8 minutes per side.

PER SERVING:
298 Calories; 24g Fat ; 19g Protein; 0g Carbohydrate; 0g Dietary Fiber; 74mg Cholesterol; 61mg Sodium. Exchanges: 2 1/2 Lean Meat; 3 Fat.

SERVING SUGGESTIONS: Grilled corn on the cob and a big hearty salad. (To grill corn on the cob, wrap it in aluminum foil, having first seasoned it with butter, salt, pepper, or however you like.)

You now have the know-how to select quality produce and good poultry and other meats. But how about finding the right fish? Don't worry—I'm not going to let you flounder. I do have a heart (or at least a sole). Yeah, I can hear you groaning as you read this—very finny, you say (groan again!).

Trying to buy good fish is pretty simple once you've located a reputable place to buy fish (could even be the fish counter at your local grocery store). When you walk in the door or up to the counter, does the place smell sharply fishy—even a little bit like ammonia? That's an indicator of not-so-fresh fish. A good place to buy fresh fish will smell fresh—there's a definite difference. You will still know you're buying fish (it won't smell like roses and lilacs in there), but it will still smell fresh and clean.

If you're at the fish case at the grocery store (in other words, it's totally self-serve), you will still need to start with the sniff test. Smell it without the plastic on, if you can. If not, you'll want to at least smell through the plastic, or try to anyway (this is, of course, assuming you're doing a self-serve thing here). Rule number one in fish buying (the fresh kind, anyway) is if it smells strongly fishy, you don't want it.

Next is how it looks. All fish should be firm (bounces back when you touch it), the flesh opaque and together (no big gaps in the flesh), and the color true (you want even coloring).

The freshness of frozen fish is harder to discern, but if you look for flash-frozen fish (especially if it was filleted and frozen on board ship), you'll get quality that is comparable (in my experience) to fresh.

Generally, it's important to know the source of any fish. When it's possible, choose wild fish over farmed fish, especially with salmon. Farm-raised fish don't get a lot of swimming room, are more prone to disease, and won't have as much Omega 3s as wild fish, an important nutrient. When Mama said fish was brain food, she was referring to wild salmon, methinks.

CHAPTER FOUR

HOW TO SLICE, DICE, AND STAND ON YOUR HEAD

One thing that you will have to add to your skill set, should you actually want to cook and quit talking about it, is some proficiency with knives. You are going to learn how to chop so you don't lose a hand or sever an artery. Isn't that a great idea?

In other words, you're not going to leave those sharp objects in the block of wood they most likely came in. No, you're gonna use 'em and learn to use them right so you won't put your eye out. And this is where we'll talk about the very mechanics of slicing and dicing so you can really use your knives. My approach is a little different in that I actually *want* you to understand what I'm saying. I don't want to impress you with fancy terms you won't remember, can't pronounce, and wouldn't want to, either. So don't be intimidated, and keep reading. Knives are cool tools, and you're just inches away from knowing how to use one like one of those guys on TV. Neat, huh?

There are a variety of ways that things need to be cut in order to be successfully used in a recipe. My favorite, of course, is your basic chop. Chopping is simple: just keep the knife going until you get what you're chopping into the size you want—big bits or little bits. No real art to it at all, but there is a definite skill to chopping. You want to be able to wield a knife and be comfortable enough with it that you can easily chop an onion in about a minute (or much less time, as your knife proficiency grows). If you're taking longer than a minute on an onion, you're either unsure of your knife skills, using the wrong knife, cutting it all wrong, or all of the above. The bottom line is, when you're lagging in certain culinary skills, your overall performance in the kitchen becomes a long, drawn-out process. What should have been a 30-minute dinner now takes an hour to prepare and you're not feeling the love for cooking anymore.

Let's remedy that, shall we? Off we go, then, to define some cutting, chopping, slicing and dicing terms, as well as tell you how to do them all easily. You gotta love that!

Chop: This is your basic chop-chop with the big knife (French knife or santoku). Although I gave you some basic knife instruction in Chapter One, you need more info, so off we go to chop. Chopping involves cutting food into pieces that are basically the same size—large, medium, or small. If no size is indicated, then it is assumed that the size is medium. However, understand that chopping is not an exact science and you're just basically trying to get the dang thing cut up. Irregularly sized pieces are just fine as long as you don't have great big pieces mixed with teeny-tiny bits. Get it?

Cube: This time, you want your chopped-up pieces to be about ½ inch in size. I don't use this term very often, but it's useful to know in case you ever use another cookbook (although that practice is highly frowned upon).

Dice: To cut food into smaller pieces than cubing, usually about ¼ inch in size. Just remember, though, that it needn't be perfect. Think small.

Julienne: This is a French term for cutting stuff into strips, finely. Kinda like a matchstick, only different. Ideally, you want the strips to be even, but for goodness' sake, don't stress over it. As a matter of fact, you won't see me use this term very much, either, because it's a pain in the neck to do, and heaven knows it's better to do strips than to invest your precious time trying to copy some fussy French terminology.

Mince: Mincing is making your chopping ultrafine, or, in terms we can all appreciate and use often, itty-bitty. Make sense? In other words, don't worry about making everything uniform in size; just make sure it's small, as in teeny-tiny.

Slice: All this means is you're cutting slices instead of pieces. So think of a tomato or onion slice on top of a burger. Naturally, you want nice, even slices if at all possible. That's a slice of what slicing looks like.

Here are some basic three-step illustrations on how to do chop and dice. Take it slow and easy.

  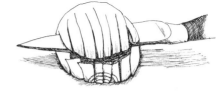

After peeling the onion, slice both ends of the onion off, and cut it in half. Place the cut side of the onion down on a cutting board. Make vertical cuts on the onion as shown in the drawing.

Now make horizontal cuts on the onion, as illustrated.

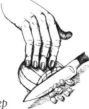

Making your "claw" with the opposing hand, carefully chop the onion with your knife hand. The claw will keep your fingers safe. This is an important principle for keeping your digits intact.

CHAPTER FIVE

HOW TO SAUTÉ, SIMMER, AND REALLY GET COOKING

Once it's time to get cookin', you gotta step into the kitchen and grab a little heat. Some heat from the stovetop, that is. When it comes to infusing food with heat (that method we cookbook authors affectionately call cooking), I am overtly fond of the skillet. This basic method of stovetop cooking will make dinner fast and easy, and make you feel like you know what you're doing (even if you're massively unsure of yourself). The trick is in controlling the heat and having a good skillet that will conduct said heat. Got that? Good, let's move on.

Once you've got the skillet by the handle, it's time to bandy about some nifty cooking terms. The word *sautéing* comes to mind. Don't let this culinary-esque word intimidate you—it's a cinch to master the sauté, I promise. Almost anything you cook—poultry, fish, other meat, vegetables, you name it—will taste better when you give it the old sauté (ice cream would be one that I wouldn't try, however). *Sauté* means "to jump" in French (I remember *sautéing* corner to corner at the ballet studio as a nubile young lass). For this particular *sauté*, you won't have to strap on toe shoes though, I promise.

So if *sauté* means "jumping," how does that translate into cooking?

Sautéing is a little like frying, only different. How's that for confusing? I once had a gal e-mail me, telling me she hated my recipes because I "fried" everything. I took great offense at her comments, giving her a mini-lecture on the joys of sautéing, yet in a way she was sorta right.

To sauté, you must use a little fat. Note the word *little*. The fat needs to be friendly to heat (definitely don't use the virgin version), the pan needs to be right (a heavy-bottomed skillet with sloped sides is ideal), and the food needs to be cut into pieces about the same size for even cooking. Once you've got those items on your sauté checklist marked off, it's time to belly up to the stovetop and get cooking.

There are those who heat the pan first and then add the oil; there are those who add the oil and heat the pan at the same time. You figure out your own sauté style, but for me, in my always seemingly rushed cooking style, I do both at the same time. Medium-high heat is good; high heat will smoke and burn your oil, and is not good.

Once the oil is hot enough and has spread in your pan (you might need to do the spreading; just pick the pan up and roll the oil around, then place it back on the heat), add your goodies. Remember not to overcrowd your pan or you'll stew rather than sauté. I found this out the hard way when cooking my fabulous beef Stroganoff for a crowd. The overcrowded skillet made for less-than-fabulous results, and I was sadly disappointed in the flavor factor (severely diminished by the stewing—it tasted watered-down). Let that be a lesson. You can batch-cook all day long, but do so in small batches and don't let your skillet get too filled up, lest your fabulous meal taste anemic, as mine did.

So there you are, you and your skillet, all heated up and ready to go. You've added the goodies; they're making delicious aromas. Now what? You need to get them moving so they won't burn. A little browning is nice, but unless you're doing Cajun, you won't want to move past brown (or you can go to caramelization; we'll talk about that in a minute). When you move things around in the pan, you need to use a spatula or tongs or a large spoon, or do it the way they do it on TV and toss it in the air. (I don't recommend this method unless your last name happens to be Lagasse.) You want all sides nicely browned.

Browning is what makes flavor, so don't be shy once you see your meat and/or veggies turning a nice golden brown. The skid marks on the bottom of your pan from these sautéed lovelies will make for a gorgeous sauce, too. Stay tuned—we'll be going there right after we talk about caramelization.

Caramelization is what happens when your heat stays consistently on the food and the browning process just keeps on keepin' on. The key is keeping the heat at about medium-high—not all the way high or back you go to a blackening effect, which is only useful in Cajun cuisine. Caramelizing releases the natural sugars of veggies. This is what happens if they are left in your pan and go past light brown (but not to Cajun). This is also why very nicely browned (also known as caramelized) onions taste so sweet. Bet you didn't know that!

On to the sauce portion of this cooking lesson. Let's pretend for a moment that you've just sautéed some chicken and veggies. The chicken is nicely cooked, as are your veggies. Pull the chicken and veggies from the pan and place on a warm plate and keep warm. (I turn my oven on to the lowest temp and then put a very loose foil tent "hat" on top of what I just sautéed. I don't tuck the sides of the foil in; just let it rest on top to preserve the heat. If you tuck it all in, it will steam and lose its sautéed appeal.) On the bottom of your pan, you're going to see all kinds of browned stuff from the chicken and veggies, or what I refer to quite often as "browned goodie bobs." This is concentrated flavor that will make for an exquisite sauce.

To make sauce, you will need liquid. I like to add chicken broth (adds more flavor and body than just plain water). I also might add a little wine, depending on what I've just cooked. The deal is that you're going to use the liquid to pull the stuff up off the bottom and incorporate it into the liquid using your trusty wire whisk. We talked about whisks way back in Chapter One, when we were discussing kitchen tools.

Anyway, you're going to crank the heat up somewhat (not too high or the liquid will all evaporate too fast), and whisk the bottom of the pan like your life depended on it. Your liquid will start to turn a little brown (from incorporating the goodie bobs), and next thing you know, you'll have something that starts to look like a sauce emerging. Now we're cooking! Isn't this the coolest? When I made my first sauce like this I felt like I could do anything in the kitchen. It's really that empowering. Really!

At this point, you may have enough liquid, too much liquid, or not enough. The remedies are simple: if it's just right, pull it from the heat, arrange your chicken and veggies on a serving plate, and pour a portion of the sauce over the top. If you have too much liquid, then bring your sauce down to a simmer (see page 53 for a detailed explanation of what a simmer should look like), and let the sauce reduce via evaporation. Now, if you let it reduce a lot, you'll make your sauce into a reduction instead (see page 54 for more of a detailed explanation), which is really just a concentrated sauce, and for our purposes right now you don't need to go there. If you don't have enough liquid, then add just a little more chicken broth (or your liquid of choice) and whisk away till you get the desired consistency.

Whew! There you have it, Sauté 101, complete with a lovely sauce. How's that for an explanation? Are you feeling good about your skillet now? I hope so. And lest you think the sauté discussion is over, it's not. As they say in commercials, wait—there's more!

Remember that I told you earlier that sautéing was related to frying, only different? You would think now that I've gone into expansive detail about sautéing that I would tell you about frying. But the thing is I won't, I can't, and it would go against everything I consider sacrosanct. In other words, frying (especially the deep-fat kind) is so dreadfully unhealthy that it would be a sin against nature and man to tell you how to do this. There are books, websites, and other people who will give you that injurious information if you insist, but I hope your conscience is so seared at this point that you'll throw away your Fry Daddy, Fry Mama, or anything else from the Fry Family taking up residence in your kitchen.

Since I won't tell you about frying, you probably want to know about using your nonstick skillet, don't you? I suppose it's natural to ask. After all, nonstick surfaces have been with us for a while and are part of most people's kitchen landscapes. I, too, am the closet owner of a nonstick skillet. I don't use it often, only employing it for limited use—for example, eggs any which way, heating tortillas, sautéing spinach, and such. Why? The biggest reason is that the nonstick surface doesn't stick, so you miss out on the opportunity to later make a sauce out of all the browned goodie bobs left in the bottom of your pan, as previously discussed. Trust me on this—you need a good stainless-steel skillet with nice sloping sides (preferably a couple of different sizes; a 10-inch and 12-inch would be good) to make wonderful meals all sauced up and ready to be served.

Now that you understand the sauté concept, let's move on. You are going to need some more terminology to add to your cooking bag of tricks. Fact is, you will be seeing these terms thrown around in just about any recipe for the rest of your cooking days. Rather than be intimidated, I want you to feel confident enough to swagger into the kitchen with a smirk on your face and an apron wrapped around your body, knowing you can sauté with the big boys and do innumerable other kitchen tasks, including using sharp objects without fear. These terms (in no particular order) will help you understand what you're doing when cooking and will help you to have more confidence in the kitchen once you've read the definition and actually performed the corresponding task. There are many more cooking terms than the ones listed below, but in my opinion, it's TMI (too much information). Besides, I figure if it's a term you really need to know, you'll e-mail me or send up a smoke signal from your house.

Simmer: When you simmer, you keep things just below the boiling point. You've even heard this term used to describe someone who was angry—they were simmering (just below the boiling point or before they threw an absolute tizzy). Simmering utilizes tiny bubbles that barely make it to the surface of whatever liquid you're simmering something in, as opposed to boiling, which is pretty darned obvious and employs much bigger bubbles. Boiling can be rather noisy, too. A rolling boil is quite evident—it rolls and boils just like you would expect a rolling boil to do.

Reductions and/or Reducing a Sauce: Reducing a sauce makes it more flavorful and thicker. You can reduce a sauce two ways: by boiling it rapidly or by simmering it a little slower. Both methods produce a richer sauce that is also known as a reduction. To make a good reduction, you should start out hotter and boil the sauce, turning it down as the sauce evaporates, or you will lose too much liquid. The size of the pan and the amount of liquid to be reduced will influence how this is done. Pay attention to these two factors and you'll get great results with your reduction sauces.

Braise: This is one of my favorite cooking methods for hearty greens (such as collards, Swiss chard, or kale) that require more cooking than a quick sauté or steam. Braising has you cooking the food slowly in a small amount of liquid in a covered pan or pot. Sautéing your food first, then braising, brings out the best of whatever it is you're braising.

Brown: We've already discussed browning in detail, but I just wanted to add that I always brown whatever it is that I am throwing in my slow-cooker, even if the recipe doesn't call for it to be browned. I might even call browning, "searing" (see *sear*, for more info). It makes a huge difference in the food's flavor. If you love your slow-cooker the way I love mine, this is a terrific hint that will help kick up your slow-cooking to the next level.

Fold: This is something you do to something that has been whipped and has a bunch of air in it. To make a meringue or a mousse (which you may actually want to attempt someday), you whip the egg whites or whipping cream till fluffy and full of air. Then you add your aerated ingredient to the bowlful of ingredients already sitting there by using a spatula and gently turning it over with the hand holding the spatula, while rotating the bowl with the other hand. It's tricky, but if you remember that you want to retain as much air in the aerated substance as possible, you won't deflate your airy element. Go easy and don't fret about it not being completely blended.

Bake: Aw, come on! I don't have to explain that one to you, do I? You know how to bake. Your mom read you the directions to your Easy-Bake oven, didn't she? Same same. All you have to do is turn your oven to bake, set the temperature, and allow it to heat up to the proper temp. This is important and is called *preheating*. (Look, I defined two terms at once! That's as good as a "buy one, get one free" sale at the grocery store.) The cool thing is, you're using a real oven and not a lightbulb to cook with. You're a grown-up now.

Broil: Hey, this one is in the oven, too. All you really need to know is that you have to allow it to preheat (just like baking). You need to position your oven rack correctly (do this *before* you start the broiler to avoid handling awkward, sizzling-hot oven racks), use a pan appropriate for the broiler (no glass ever!), and then, once you put your food under the broiler, watch it like a hawk watches a rabbit in a field. You'll need to pounce at the right time, pulling it out of the broiler, or it will get away from you, setting off the smoke alarm and turning dinner into a burnt offering.

Baste: I don't recommend basting. Ever. There is no earthly good reason to baste anything. Basting steals the heat, doesn't improve the flavor, and causes you to cook something longer than you should (see *Saving Dinner for the Holidays*, where I really get into my anti-basting diatribe with the Thanksgiving turkey). However, since this is a basic-type cookbook, I am obliged to at least tell you what it is. Basting is (supposedly) moistening while cooking. To baste, you must open the oven incessantly (letting out precious heat and causing whatever it is that is cooking to need extra cooking time), and, using a bulb baster (looks like an eye dropper for Godzilla), suck the cooking juices from the bottom of the pan, and squirt them over the top of whatever it is that whomever it is thinks needs to be basted. The sad fact is that whatever is going through this futile basting exercise has already been sealed shut from the initial cooking process (there's a little kitchen science thrown in for free). Think I'm a little biased about basting?

Sear: This is something you will do first to your meat before it hits the slow-cooker. It's merely subjecting your poultry or other meat to very high heat to seal in the juices and add a nicely browned crust to the outside of the poultry or other meat. Searing is good; basting is bad. Got that?

Stew: I know we talked about this when we discussed in detail the art of the sauté. However, I didn't tell you that sometimes stewing is good—as when making beef stew, for example. All stewing is, essentially, cooking something (usually a tougher piece of meat) in a liquid for a long time to make it tender. This is why you always use tougher pieces of meat in a beef stew or pot roast. Using tender meat will give you an untender result when you stew.

Truss: This is something I don't think you should do. It's unnatural and unnerving to do unless you're into poultry bondage. Trussing is tying up a bird with some cooking twine so it doesn't lose its shape while roasting in the oven. Who cares? It's dead, you're cooking it, and you're going to eat it, so to heck with trussing. Trust me on this one . . . there are better uses of your time and twine.

CHAPTER SIX

TIMING IS EVERYTHING

Once you have the general idea of how to use a knife (and that is generally where you start with most cooking unless you're baking), you will need to know how to time a meal and coordinate your cooking efforts. It's not as hard as you think—it just requires a little forethought.

You need a starting place, once you've chosen a recipe to cook. I learned a long time ago while cooking in a restaurant kitchen that putting together a *mise-en-place* (pronounced *meez ahn plahs*) before you start to cook will save you a ton of time. This little French term means literally "to put in place."

So what the heck is a *mise-en-place*? It is simply a gathering together of the things you're going to need to make that particular recipe. For example, if I am cooking on television or cooking for an event, I have all the ingredients measured, chopped, and sitting in little see-through bowls ready to go. The spoons, spatulas, pans, and other cooking implements will all likewise be standing at attention, waiting to be utilized. That is my professional, TV, I'm-ready-for-my-close-up *mise-en-place*.

Now, you could do your *mise-en-place* that way if you want, or you could do a modified version of this like I do at home, which means: just get the stuff out that you're going to need, chop the onions, open the can of tomatoes, get out the skillet, etc. I don't recommend the little see-through-bowl method unless you're expecting a film crew to pop over to your house while you're making dinner—too much cleanup.

Cleanup on Aisle Four!

Let's face it. One of the hassles with cooking is that there is always cleanup that needs to be attended to. Not facing the mess during the cooking ensures that you will have a massive amount to do after the cooking.

The way to take the edge off some of that cleanup is to keep a sink full of hot sudsy water and throw everything (except sharp objects) in the mix. It will then take you only a minute to wipe down the countertops, put stuff back in the fridge, etc., and clean up what is in that soapy water.

I consider cleaning my kitchen after a meal to be a two-step process. The first step is done during and directly after making the meal. Then after you've served dinner, there is a secondary, faster cleanup. Doing dishes this way saves you from the dread of cleaning up a colossally messy kitchen of Thanksgiving proportions.

You've done this *mise-en-place* thing yourself many times, but you just never knew it. Ever make a sandwich? You get the bread out, the condiments, meats, cheeses, etc. You get the knife out of the drawer and even the plate to put the sandwich on once it's assembled. See there? You've been there, done that, made the sandwich, and didn't even know you were a *mise-en-place* expert already, by golly. Keeping the sandwich pre-assembly mind-set for all your cooking is going to help you tremendously for anything you attempt in the kitchen.

So you've assembled your modified *mise-en-place* according to what you're making for dinner. Now you need to figure out your timing. Let's say you're making a skillet chicken recipe for dinner. You have side dishes of steamed broccoli, baked potatoes, and a salad—all need making as well as the entrée. Getting everything on the table at the same time requires good timing. To figure this out, you simply need to be able to count, know what is going to take the longest, and start there.

A good starting place is always reading the recipe thoroughly. I know

I'm repeating myself, but this is important. I can't tell you how many times novice (and not so novice) cooks neglect this important step. Not only will neglecting this mess up your timing, but you could be in for a surprise or two along the way. With my Saving Dinner books, I often give a do-ahead tip (like marinating the chicken overnight) so you know up front what to expect, but not all recipes are created equal—you can't count on knowing up front what you are going to need.

After you've read the recipe, you need to figure out which food item will take the longest to cook. It should go without saying that a menu that requires every dish to be made at the last minute will be very difficult to accomplish, especially for the newbie cook. But back to our make-believe menu of skillet chicken, baked potatoes, steamed broccoli, and a salad. Which menu item is going to need the most cooking? If you said the baked potatoes, you're the grand prize winner—come on down! The potatoes will clearly require the most cooking time. So getting those potatoes cleaned, prepped, and popped into the oven is first up. Once you have the taters in the oven, you will most likely want to start on the skillet chicken (but don't do all the cooking—just prep it). These types of recipes usually require cooking the chicken in the skillet for several minutes on each side. During the initial prep time, you can prepare the broccoli (as in wash it, cut it up, and put it in the steamer ready to go—not cook it), put together your salad, and even set the table. Being able to get dinner (or any other meal) on the table fast is all about timing and multitasking at the appropriate times. In other words, you don't want to be multitasking when you should be stirring a sauce that needs to be stirred constantly—unless you want less-than-optimal results with an irregularly stirred sauce, that is.

Dinner Party 101

So you're feeling good and you wanna try your skills out on your first dinner party, do you? The very word *entertaining* can be hugely intimidating, conjuring up images of lavish spreads, immaculately appointed homes, and other visions of magazine living. It is time to get a reality check and get to the heart of the matter.

First off, let's chuck the word *entertaining*. You need to remember that it's not about slick magazine spreads, but rather about enjoying the hospitality of good friends by breaking bread together.

Your first foray into a dinner party should be very basic and simple, keeping the hospitality mind-set firmly in place. Hospitality isn't something that one is talented in and another is not—it is something that is cultivated, much like a plant. All it takes is a welcoming home, a good meal (I can help you with that), and a warm and welcoming attitude (that's your department).

If you're going to practice hospitality, you need to keep your perspective. Don't invite someone who will intimidate you the first time around. You need allies at this time—comrades, *amigos.* You don't need to be intimidated as you take your first baby steps at hospitality.

The first rule is to keep it simple. Let me say that again. The first rule is keeping it simple. *Way* simple. I would suggest a big slow-cooker filled with some terrific chili, a big green salad, some cornbread, and some good friends to enjoy it with you. The kind of friends that you ask to bring dessert—that's the type of guest you want for your first entertaining/hospitality venture.

Grab some flowers and throw them in a pitcher for a country effect. Set the table with some red-and-white-checked napkins or tablecloth and you're good to go. Don't kill yourself over decorating. Simple is necessary *and* smart.

Here is a recipe that I should be ashamed to share because it's so easy. But I'm not. It's good enough for company even—enjoy!

Really Easy Mixed-Bean Chili

Serves 6 (easily doubled to serve more)

1 (16-ounce) can pinto beans, rinsed and drained
1 (16-ounce) can black beans, rinsed and drained
1 (2-ounce) package taco seasoning mix — 1/2 PKG
1 (8-ounce) jar salsa (your favorite) — MILD
1 (10-ounce) package frozen corn kernels
1 large sweet potato, peeled and cubed (this makes the recipe special)

Can be too spicy!

Dump all the ingredients into a slow-cooker, set on low, and cook for 6 to 8 hours. Mix well before serving. How hard is that??

PER SERVING:

283 Calories; 1g Fat; 15g Protein; 55g Carbohydrate; 15g Dietary Fiber; 0mg Cholesterol; 584mg Sodium. Exchanges: 3 Grain (Starch); 1/2 Lean Meat; 1/2 Vegetable; 0 Other Carbohydrates.

SERVING SUGGESTIONS: Serve with your favorite corn bread (make or buy), a great big salad, and dessert. (If your friends don't bring it, how about make-your-own ice cream sundaes?)

CHAPTER SEVEN

THE JOY OF THE DINNER TABLE

T his is the place where I stop teaching and start meddling. Put up with me for a minute while I take off my apron and stand in my pulpit. Telling people about the importance of the family dinner table is my mission in life, so sit down, buckle up, and listen. Here we go—

I am passionate about that sweet word *Dinner*! And I like to hear it hollered loudly, followed by the thundering sound of kids stampeding to the table. This is the echo of real human beings taking the opportunity to not only break bread together but also to connect heart-to-heart.

Sitting down for dinner as a family has almost become the exception and not the rule, sadly. The family table has been sacrificed for various activities, and the results are disheartening. Numerous studies have shown the devastating effects of this lost familial art: children don't do as well in school and have more of a propensity toward alcohol, sex, and drugs (keep reading for more details). Because of our busyness, many family members feel disconnected from one another, children are non-communicative, and the opportunity to really know and care about one another is gone in the quest to get to soccer practice on time.

A little thing like trying to sit down together as a family for dinner every night will have an impact on the family like almost nothing else. For a lot of families, this could be the only time in the day that it is possible to connect with one another.

QUESTION: How do you do that?
ANSWER: It depends!

There is no easy, pat, one-answer-fits-all. I've noticed that my answer has evolved as my children and I have gotten older. My children are teenagers now, but when they were younger, I reworked my schedule so that they were part of the dinnertime preparation and routine. Not only did I discover some additional time to develop a good relationship with them, but I also taught them cooking skills and they learned about nutrition because they were "doing" nutrition in the kitchen. This early training will serve them for life, I am convinced. Though they don't always make the healthiest choices (it's harder when they get older and have a little more autonomy!), they make much better choices than most of their peers—by putting limits on soft drinks when they're out, for example.

Here are some scary statistics to help you grasp how much is riding on this simple piece of family culture:

- CASA's (National Center on Addiction and Substance Abuse at Columbia University) 1998 Teen Survey found that teens who ate dinner with their parents twice a week or less were four times more likely to smoke cigarettes, three times more likely to smoke marijuana, and nearly twice as likely to drink as those who ate dinner with their parents six or seven times a week.

- CASA's 1999 Teen Survey found that teens from families that almost never ate dinner together were 72 percent likelier than the average teen to use illegal drugs, cigarettes, and alcohol; while those from families that almost always ate dinner together were 31 percent less likely than the average teen to engage in those activities.

- Research by other organizations has shown that teens who frequently eat family dinners with their parents are less likely than other teens to have sex at young ages, get into fights, or be suspended from school, and are at lower risk for thoughts of suicide. Frequent family dining is also correlated with doing well in school and developing healthy eating habits. This pattern holds true regardless of a teen's gender, family structure, or socioeconomic level.

CASA is primarily a think tank dedicated to finding out how to prevent drug and alcohol abuse among children. Their findings prompted the establishment of Family Day and the above-mentioned statistics. They offer more information on their website than I have given. Check them out at *www.casafamilyday.org.*

I invite you to take this information to heart. Not to make you feel guilty. Not to promote my books or website. But to give you some significant food for thought to help you understand that, underneath everything that you do (or don't do), someone is watching you, emulating you, and wanting more than ever to connect with you. Your family dinner table is the starting place for making this happen. Don't ever underestimate the power of dinner.

Okay, apron back on. Let's get back to work. Now we need to talk about setting that table, creating a mood, and all that jazz.

READY, SET, GO!

Cooking is one thing, setting a nice table is another thing. I am astounded at how many times I've asked people to set the table for me (guests, friends, relatives) and they didn't know how to do it properly. Setting a table isn't nearly as difficult as trying to truss a chicken (which I try to avoid at all costs), but you can't avoid setting the table unless you go Neanderthal style and just fling everything on the table, each caveman for himself. I don't like that approach—I find it rather barbaric—and I am going to bet that you as an individual living in the civilized world don't, either. You do need to know what goes where to escape the helter-skelter look. Here's a primer on basic table setting.

To start with, I place everything I am going to use for the meal in the middle of the table, like salt and pepper, butter, sour cream, etc., so that it is easily reachable and reasonably laid out. (You don't want it to look like a three-year-old pitched it there.) Place your condiments, sauces, etc., in little serving dishes or ramekins as appropriate. Containers of sour cream, jars of salsa, and the like look tacky on your table. I remember going to a dinner party once where the hostess plopped down a pot—as in the pot they were cooked in—of beans in the middle of the table. The mashed potatoes were likewise still in their cooking implement. I had to conscientiously restrain myself from letting my jaw drop. Let that be a lesson to you: what you cook in is not what you serve in. That's why serving dishes, platters, and the like were created. Got that? Good. Now let's set the table.

If you're going to have people serve themselves (family style, with the food in the middle of the table, on suitable serving dishes), then you will want to lay down the dinner plates first (unless you want to use a tablecloth or place mats—in that case, lay those down first). If you are going to plate the food first in the kitchen, then stack your dinner plates next to the stovetop or wherever else is convenient once the plating begins. But let's go back to the table. Plates should be placed about 2 inches from the table's edge, or thereabouts. For heaven's sake, don't measure it to make sure you've got your compulsory 2 inches, lest people mistake you for a perfectionist. (And if you're a perfectionist, this book is not for you, so close it now and give it to one of your less than perfect friends. They will appreciate the imperfect help.)

At this point, I would set the silverware, as it will determine better placement for the rest of stuff. Forks are placed to the left of the dinner plate and the dinner fork is closest to the plate. You will place the salad fork first on the far left, then the dinner fork if doing courses. In our household, we use the dinner fork for dinner and salad (gasp!). The reason I do this is because we have salad *with* our dinner. If I served the salad first, I would use two forks. There. Feel better now? Unless you're truly hard-core about the silverware, I think I just redeemed myself. If you still need a moment, breathe into a paper bag. Listen, there is more to life than anxiety attacks over fork etiquette.

Next is the knife. Knife blades should be placed with the edge toward the dinner plate. The butter knife should go on the bread and butter plate, if you're having bread and butter. If not, forgo the bread and butter plate and skip the butter knife as well (seems elementary, but I've seen tables set without b&b plates and yet the butter knife was present. Go figure).

The salad plate goes left and up (see picture below). The wineglass (and doesn't everyone's dinner deserve a nice glass of wine?) goes to the right of the water glass (which is perched right above the knife). If you had more than one wineglass, you would arrange them in a triangular shape, with the water glass at the bottom point of said triangle. If you're doing a dinner party that fancy, I highly doubt you'd be reading this book, however. Anyway, the only thing left is the napkin. You have two choices with it—either place it under the fork or to the left of the fork. I am in favor of under the fork because of the space factor on the table. You don't have the whole table for one place setting, for heaven's sake.

So now that you have your dinner table set, let's address those times when you're fresh out of everything (time, imagination, and ingredients) and yet your trusty fridge still holds a carton full of eggs. Eggs make for a great breakfast and an even more wonderful dinner.

When my kids were little and the eggs from our chickens were abundant, we had breakfast for dinner often. To add to the pleasure of this surprise meal, I would sometimes serve orange juice in wineglasses, light candles, and let Vivaldi wail on the stereo. That was a different era, it seems, but created treasured memories with my elementary school–age kids, for sure.

Here are some great recipes to have your own breakfast for dinner or breakfast whenever—just make sure you crank up the Vivaldi; it's perfect music to eat breakfast by.

CRUSTLESS BROCCOLI QUICHE

½ cup shredded Swiss cheese
¼ cup shredded low-fat cheddar cheese
½ cup chopped frozen broccoli, thawed
¼ cup chopped onion
¼ cup sliced mushrooms
5 eggs
½ cup skim milk
½ cup half-and-half
Nutmeg to taste
Pepper to taste

Preheat oven to 375°F. Lightly grease a 9-inch pie pan.

Spread cheese on bottom of pan and top with vegetables.

Whisk together eggs, milk, half-and-half, nutmeg, and pepper. Pour over cheese and vegetables. Bake about 45 minutes or until knife inserted in center comes out clean; let stand (rest) 10 minutes before slicing. Slice and serve.

PER SERVING:
121 Calories; 8g Fat; 9g Protein; 4g Carbohydrate; 1g Dietary Fiber; 169mg Cholesterol; 109mg Sodium. Exchanges: 1 Lean Meat; 1/2 Vegetable; 0 Nonfat Milk; 1 Fat.

CRUSTLESS CRAB QUICHE

Serves 4–6

1 tablespoon olive oil
½ cup chopped onion
4 cups coarsely chopped fresh spinach
⅛ teaspoon dried tarragon
⅛ teaspoon ground nutmeg
Salt and pepper to taste
1 (8-ounce) can crabmeat, drained
¾ cup grated Swiss cheese
1 cup low-fat milk
5 eggs, lightly beaten

Preheat oven to 375°F. Lightly grease a 9-inch pie pan.

In a skillet, heat olive oil over medium-high heat. Add onion; sauté 4 minutes or until onion is translucent. Add spinach and spices, cooking about 2 minutes or until spinach wilts.

Arrange spinach mixture in the bottom of the pie pan. Place crabmeat over the top of the spinach, and then add the cheese.

In a bowl, combine milk and eggs, blending well with a whisk. Pour over spinach mixture. Bake for 30 to 45 minutes or until a knife inserted in center comes out clean; let stand (rest) 10 minutes before slicing.

PER SERVING:
178 Calories; 10g Total Fat; 17g Protein; 1g Dietary Fiber; 4g Carbohydrate; 206mg Cholesterol; 238mg Sodium. Food Exchanges: 0 Grain (Starch); 2 Lean Meat; 1/2 Vegetable; 0 Fruit; 1 Fat; 0 Other Carbohydrates.

HASH BROWN QUICHE

3 cups shredded peeled potatoes
¼ cup (½ stick) butter, melted
1 cup shredded low-fat cheddar cheese
1 cup shredded Monterey Jack cheese
1 cup diced turkey ham
½ cup skim milk
2 eggs
Salt and pepper to taste

Preheat oven to 425°F. Lightly grease a 9-inch pie pan.

Press potatoes into pan to form a crust. Brush with melted butter. Bake 25 minutes. Reduce oven temperature to 350°F and remove pan from oven.

Fill crust with cheeses and turkey ham. Whisk together milk, eggs, and salt and pepper. Pour into pan and bake 30 to 40 minutes or until knife inserted in center comes out clean. Rest and serve.

PER SERVING:
276 Calories; 18g Fat; 13g Protein; 16g Carbohydrate; 1g Dietary Fiber; 100mg Cholesterol; 615mg Sodium. Exchanges: 1 Grain (Starch); 1 1/2 Lean Meat; 0 Nonfat Milk; 2 1/2 Fat.

FABULOUS FRITTATA

Serves 4–6

8 ounces fresh turkey sausage, sliced
2 cups shredded unpeeled zucchini
2 green onions, sliced
½ teaspoon dried basil
1 teaspoon Italian seasoning
4 eggs
⅓ cup low-fat milk
4 ounces low-fat cream cheese, diced into ½-inch cubes
1 cup shredded mozzarella cheese
1 cup shredded sharp cheddar cheese

Preheat oven to 325°F. Lightly grease an 8-inch pie pan or quiche pan.

Brown sausage in a skillet over medium heat and drain well. Spread over bottom of pan. Layer zucchini over sausage, then sprinkle green onions and seasonings on top.

Whisk eggs with milk and pour over zucchini and sausage. Sprinkle with cream cheese cubes. Top with mozzarella and cheddar cheeses. Bake for 45 minutes or until top is lightly golden or knife inserted in center comes out clean. Let stand (rest) 10 minutes and serve.

PER SERVING:
243 Calories; 18g Fat; 16g Protein; 5g Carbohydrate; 1g Dietary Fiber; 192mg Cholesterol; 378mg Sodium. Exchanges: 0 Grain (Starch); 2 Lean Meat; 1/2 Vegetable; 0 Nonfat Milk; 2 1/2 Fat; 0 Other Carbohydrates.

BASIC CHEESE STRATA

Serves 4–6

6 eggs, beaten
2 cups milk
Salt and pepper
1 tablespoon Dijon mustard
6 slices whole wheat bread
3 cups shredded low-fat cheddar cheese

Lightly grease a 2-quart casserole dish.

Mix eggs, milk, salt and pepper to taste, and mustard. Set aside.

Cut bread into cubes. Place a layer of bread, followed by a layer of cheese, in casserole dish. Repeat layers until bread and cheese are all used.

Pour egg mixture over bread. Cover and refrigerate overnight or for at least 1 to 2 hours to allow egg to soak into bread.

Preheat oven to 350°F.

Bake uncovered for 45 minutes or until light and fluffy. Serve warm.

OPTION 1—TEX-MEX STRATA: Add 1 (4-ounce) can green chilies, drained and chopped, and 2 tablespoons finely minced onion to the egg mixture. Substitute Monterey Jack cheese for cheddar and proceed with the recipe.

OPTION 2—SPRING ASPARAGUS STRATA: Add about 10 asparagus spears that have been steamed, cooled, and chopped, along with 6 ounces chopped ham to the egg mixture. Substitute provolone cheese for cheddar and proceed with the recipe.

OPTION 3—SPINACH STRATA: Add 5 ounces lightly sautéed fresh baby spinach (sauté in a little butter and olive oil, salt and pepper to taste) to the egg mixture. Substitute Gruyère or Swiss for cheddar and proceed with the recipe.

PER SERVING (BASED ON 6 SERVINGS):
270 Calories; 11g Fat; 25g Protein; 19g Carbohydrate; 2g Dietary Fiber; 202mg Cholesterol; 652mg Sodium. Exchanges: 1 Grain (Starch); 2 1/2 Lean Meat; 1/2 Nonfat Milk; 1 Fat; 0 Other Carbohydrates.

Here is my famous pancake mix. Whip up a big batch of this and keep it in a large plastic storage container in the pantry. Instructions for making pancakes and waffles included.

LEANNE'S PANCAKE MIX

Makes more than 3 quarts

8 cups flour (*if you'd like a whole-wheat mix, use whole-wheat pastry flour from health food stores*)

1½ cups buckwheat flour (*available in health food stores*)

½ cup cornmeal (*preferably stone-ground*)

1½ cups oatmeal (*blend in your blender till powdered*)

2 cups buttermilk powder (*in baking section of grocery store*)

5 tablespoons baking powder

2 tablespoons baking soda

1 cup sugar (*or Sucanat—natural sugar available in health food stores*)

2 tablespoons salt

Mix all ingredients in a very large bowl and pour into a large plastic storage container. Mark the date with a Sharpie pen on the container and store in your pantry.

TO MAKE PANCAKES OR WAFFLES:

1 cup pancake mix

½ to ⅔ cup water (*start with the lesser amount first and add if you need to*)

1 egg

2 tablespoons vegetable oil

In a medium bowl, combine pancake mix with water, egg, and vegetable oil. Heat your griddle and make your pancakes as usual! To make waffles, double the batter and follow the directions for your waffle iron.

CHAPTER EIGHT

TOOL TIME: USING YOUR TOOLS EVEN MORE

I said earlier that I've never met a kitchen store I didn't love. It's true—these places are like the proverbial toy store to me; it just doesn't get much better or more fun. I love to stroll down the aisles, checking out the latest and greatest. I adore picking up all of the assorted thingamabobs and playing with them. Sometimes you have to guess what they are and their use, but still it's quite amusing. The trick is to keep your head about you and just look. I hate to say this, but you really don't need a good portion of the stuff in there.

Temper that with the fact that there are some terrific helps out there for the home cook. And when it comes to significant help, small appliances can revolutionize the way you cook. Some of the average appliances that you have sitting in your own kitchen may need to be seen with new eyes.

That isn't just a slow-cooker hiding in the dark corner of your kitchen cabinet. That's a cook who'll be whipping up something fabulous for you and your family while you're running around all day or are at work. Do you see why you need to yank that thing out from the netherworld of your cupboard?

And the bread machine you got as a wedding gift? Your own personal baker! The freezer? A virtual restaurant waiting to be heated up. Your food processor? Your own personal kitchen assistant.

What more could a cook ask for? Every one of these tools gets neglected from time to time, but if you use them, you'll find yourself able to do so much more in the kitchen and it will be so much easier to cook. With a little bit of planning, some good recipes (got 'em right here!), and a willingness to try something new, your kitchen will never be the same.

Besides, you can tell everyone you have a full kitchen staff . . . and if you own a dishwasher, don't forget that you have a maid, too!

Domestic Appliance Checklist

Let's take a look at some of the stuff in the Dinner Diva's kitchen, which, it should be noted, is rather spare in cooking implements (plug-ins and otherwise) considering what she does for a living. These apparatuses are here because they either do one job well and better than anything else, or they are efficient multi-taskers. Here then, The List, and it's a short one:

1. *Mixer.* God bless KitchenAid for coming up with their heavy-duty (and heavy to lift, I might add) stand mixer. In order to mix well, you need some horsepower behind the metal, or watts (as in 325 watts, more or less, depending on your model). Power is what separates a great mixer from a not-so-great mixer. This contraption can whip cream and egg whites in a flash, knead a few loaves of bread, mix anything worth mixing, and look incredibly cool at the same time. I have a standard-issue white KitchenAid, but you can get them in pretty much any color, including different metallics like nickel and chrome. A must for any kitchen. Comes with a whip for whipping, a paddle for mixing, and a dough hook for kneading. You can get other attachments, including a pasta roller and a meat grinder.

2. *Griddle.* I may not use this often, but when I do, I am very happy I have it. The griddle I am fond of is a large one that can cook a pound of bacon at a time, all plugged in and sitting on my countertop. There is a little hole in the griddle and a cup, too, to catch the hot drippings. After the bacon has been cooked, the nonstick surface is cleaned up (easily) and a boatload of pancake making can ensue. Big griddles help you make big lumberjack-size breakfasts and will allow you to brown and cook food for a dozen in no time flat. If you intend to ever

have a bunch of people over at any given time for a meal, chances are you will haul this appliance out and use it over and over again.

3. *Blender and food processor.* Yeah, they were mentioned earlier in the book, but I do need to mention them again, especially considering the lovely blender/food processor recipes for sauces I have here. All of these wonderful sauces take mere minutes to make and can dress up a plain-Jane piece of chicken in a hurry.

4. *Mini–food processor.* Need a quick chop or a blend for something small? The mini–food processor is excellent for this job, weighs less than a cheesecake, and can do all kinds of breathtaking things like chop nuts or hard veggies and make a quickie pesto. I love my little guy, and I suggest you get one and love yours, too.

5. *Coffeemaker and grinder.* I don't have a combo appliance, but I put them together because in my mind you cannot make a decent cup of joe unless you grind your own beans. I have been grinding my own for well over 20 years now, and every morning (that I am home, at least) I perform the same ritual of grinding, brewing, and drinking a divine cup of morning brew. I make it stronger than most people (opting for 2 tablespoons vs. 1 tablespoon of coffee per 6 ounces of water), and I have my first cup by itself, my second with my morning cereal. My coffee is exquisitely important to me (ask anyone who knows me!), and making it well requires two good appliances: a grinder and a good coffeemaker. I have a Cuisinart coffeemaker that beeps when it's ready (you gotta love that!) and does a fine job all the way around the block.

Speaking of blenders and food processors, check out the following easy recipes. See why I love them?

BLENDER HOLLANDAISE

Makes approximately 1 cup

> *4 egg yolks*
> *1 tablespoon lemon juice*
> *1 tablespoon water*
> *3 drops hot sauce (like Tabasco)*
> *½ pound (2 sticks) butter, melted*

Place egg yolks, lemon juice, water, and hot sauce in blender or food processor and purée or process for about 30 seconds. Slowly stream butter into blender or food processor while continuing to process and watch your pretty hollandaise emerge! Shut off the motor when done or it will overprocess. Not good. Use immediately.

BLENDER BERNAISE

Makes approximately 1¼ cups

> *3 egg yolks*
> *2 tablespoons lemon juice*
> *Salt and pepper*
> *1 onion slice*
> *3 sprigs parsley*
> *1 teaspoon dried tarragon*
> *2 tablespoons dry white wine*
> *⅔ cup (10 tablespoons) butter, melted*

Place all ingredients except butter in blender or food processor. Purée or process for a few seconds on low. Slowly add butter while continuing to process until thick or about another 3 minutes. Serve immediately.

BLENDER HOT SAUCE

Makes approximately 3½ cups

1 onion, chopped

1 bell pepper, de-ribbed, stemmed, and chopped

2 fresh green chilies, seeds removed (Anaheim or jalapeños, for
   example)

5 garlic cloves, pressed

1 (28-ounce) can diced tomatoes

1 teaspoon ground cumin

¾ teaspoon cayenne pepper or to taste

1 teaspoon dried oregano

3 tablespoons chopped fresh cilantro

Salt

Combine all ingredients in blender or food processor. Purée or
process until smooth. Transfer the sauce to a saucepan and simmer on
low heat, uncovered, for about 30 minutes. Stir often.

Hot sauce will keep for about 2 weeks, refrigerated and tightly covered.

BLENDER SPINACH SAUCE

Makes approximately 2 cups

1 cup chopped fresh spinach

2 tablespoons olive oil

½ cup low-fat plain yogurt

2 cloves crushed garlic

1 teaspoon dried basil

1 handful chopped parsley

1 lemon, juiced

2 tablespoons crumbled feta cheese, plus extra for top

Combine all ingredients except cheese in blender or food processor.
Purée or process till thick. Add a bit of water to thin, if necessary. Pour
sauce over food (pasta, meat, etc.) adding a little more feta cheese before serving.

BLENDER LOW-FAT ALFREDO SAUCE

Makes 1¾ cups

½ cup cubed low-fat cream cheese
1 cup low-fat milk
3 tablespoons grated Parmesan cheese
1 garlic clove, pressed
1 tablespoon white pepper
Salt

Place all ingredients in blender or food processor. Purée or process until smooth.

Transfer sauce to saucepan to warm, then pour over freshly cooked pasta. Toss and serve.

BLENDER MAYO

Makes approximately 1½ cups

1 egg
1½ tablespoons lemon juice
1 cup vegetable oil

Place the egg and lemon juice in blender or food processor.

Purée or process at a high speed until the mixture goes from yellow to white. Slowly add the oil and keep processing till you get mayo. Store in fridge.

BLENDER HUMMUS

Makes approximately 1½ cups

> 1 (15-ounce) can garbanzo beans, drained
> 4 lemons, juiced
> 1 teaspoon Asian sesame oil
> 3 garlic cloves, pressed
> Salt

Place ingredients in blender or food processor. Process or purée until smooth. If too thick, add a little water—1 to 2 teaspoons at a time—until desired consistency. Serve with veggies and pita bread. Keep refrigerated till used.

BLENDER BEAN DIP

Makes appoximately 2½ cups

> 2 (15-ounce) cans black beans, drained
> 1 onion, chopped coarsely
> 2 garlic cloves, pressed
> ½ (9-ounce) jar roasted red peppers in water, drained
> 1 cup low-sodium chicken broth
> 2 tablespoons balsamic vinegar
> Cayenne pepper
> 1 tablespoon lime juice

Place all ingredients in blender or food processor. Process or purée until smooth or desired consistency. Serve with tortilla chips and veggies.

BLENDER GUACAMOLE

Makes approximately ¾ cup

3 avocados, peeled and pitted
2 tablespoons grated onion
1¼ tablespoons lemon juice
½ teaspoon chili powder
1 ripe tomato

Place ingredients in blender or food processor. Purée or process until smooth or desired consistency. Serve with tortilla chips.

BLENDER TAPENADE

Makes approximately 1½ cups

1 cup pitted Kalamata olives
½ cup olive oil
2 garlic cloves, pressed
2 tablespoons drained capers
1 cup fresh parsley

Place ingredients in blender or food processor. Purée or process until smooth or desired consistency. Serve with crackers or bread.

BLENDER PESTO

Makes 1½ cups

2 cups basil leaves
¾ cup olive oil
¼ cup pine nuts
2 garlic cloves, pressed
Salt and pepper
¾ cup grated Romano cheese

Place ingredients in blender or food processor. Purée or process until smooth or desired consistency. Use on grilled fish or chicken.

PART TWO

RECIPE READY

CHAPTER NINE

THE SOUP AND SALAD BAR

I f I were to confess a pet peeve in the cooking department of life, it would have to be those nasty, gelatinous, condensed canned soups that not only become "soup" when heated with a corresponding can of water but also become the base for casseroles, sauces, and other deplorable "cuisine." I suppose that if I find these horrid cans of soup so annoying, it should also be a part of my mission in life to make this type of cooking unnecessary.

So on with that mission, then. Great soup doesn't have to sit simmering on the stove for hours and can, in fact, be whipped up pretty darn fast. Everyone loves a good bowl of soup, and this is something very simple that even the most novice cook can pull off.

My idea of soup is that it is a meal, not a first course. A first course is fine if you have a butler, but for the rest of us workaday stiffs, we'll take our bowls of hearty soup on a cold day, some nice hot bread, and a green salad and call it dinner.

It takes a few easy techniques previously discussed in this book: dicing an onion, chopping some vegetables, and sautéing. Easy stuff, but the results don't look easy and they look like you've got this cooking thing down pat. I love that about soups—they look so complicated but take nothing to do.

The first step to fabulous soup is having soup stock (also known as broth). Because this is a basic skills–type cookbook, I feel obligated to show you how to make a good stock—a good chicken stock and a couple of others, although I rarely fuss with any other stock. Unless you're wanting to ramp up your skills into the Wolfgang Puck stratosphere, I suggest you do the same. There truly is no need to even discuss beef stock, let alone *glace de viande*; however, I did include a recipe for it (beef stock, that is) in case you don't happen to be of the same ilk.

The sad truth is that I don't make homemade stock much these days because I'm just too darn busy and there are plenty of suitable, already made stocks that you can avail yourself of (the trick is buying the low-sodium versions—much better than the saltier editions). That said, I would be positively guilt-ridden without including a very easy recipe I've used for years. Your grandmother probably made something similar during the Great Depression, but I promise you this doesn't taste like Shoe Leather Soup.

To make this recipe, you must first have the chicken carcass handy from My Fabulous Roast Chicken recipe (page 140). Hey, I never said "Let's make stock now!" Go make yourself a chicken and come back when you have a picked-over bony carcass in your possession.

HOMEMADE CHICKEN BROTH

Makes approximately 1 quart

> *1 carcass from My Fabulous Roast Chicken (page 140)*
> *1 large onion, cut in half*
> *2 large carrots, cut in 3 pieces each (or just break them with your hands)*
> *1 large celery stalk, broken in half*
> *6 cups cold water*
> *Salt and pepper to taste*

Throw all ingredients into a large pot. Boil the daylights out of the carcass just for a minute, then turn it down to a simmer (you know how to do that) and simmer for approximately 1 hour. Let sit for 15 minutes or so and then strain with a mesh strainer. You may have some funky residual stuff sneak through doing it this way, but to get it absolutely clear, you'll need to mess with cheesecloth and all that. Do you really want to go there? Don't get obsessive—this is soup stock, for heaven's sake.

Refrigerate the strained stock after it has cooled. In a couple of hours or overnight, once the fat has risen to the top, skim it off and throw it away. Now it's ready to use!

Okay, now that you have my chicken stock recipe (and it's a good one), I thought you'd need a few more just for the sake of having them. No pressure to actually make them if you have found some decent already prepared broths in your local grocery store.

Here are some of my recipes for other stocks I can vouch for, although rarely use.

VEGETABLE STOCK

Makes approximately 2½ quarts

> *1 onion, roughly chopped*
> *8 garlic cloves, cut in half*
> *3 carrots, roughly chopped*
> *1 leek, rinsed and roughly chopped (see instructions for cutting a leek on page 88)*
> *2 celery stalks, roughly chopped*
> *2 tablespoons olive oil*
> *8 sprigs parsley*
> *2 teaspoons dried thyme*
> *Salt and pepper to taste*
> *3 quarts water*
> *1–2 bay leaves*
> *1 potato, quartered*
> *1 turnip, roughly chopped*

In a large skillet over medium heat, sauté onion, garlic, carrots, leek, and celery in olive oil for a couple of minutes. Add the parsley, thyme, salt, and pepper. Continue cooking until onion and carrots are tender, about 6 to 8 minutes.

Transfer sautéed vegetables to a large stockpot. Add water and bay leaves.

Add remaining vegetables and bring to a boil. Lower heat and simmer for 30 to 45 minutes. Sometimes when stock is simmering, the surface tends to get foamy; simply skim that off.

Once all vegetables are tender, remove stock from heat and allow to cool a wee bit. Strain stock to remove vegetables from broth. Stock is ready for immediate use. If not using right away, store in refrigerator for up to 4 days or freeze for up to 2 months.

Cut the root end off the leek, then remove the tough green leaves. You just want the white part of the leek remaining.

Using a paring knife, carefully split the white part open lengthwise exposing the many layers.

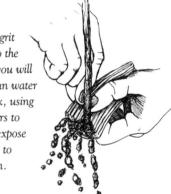

Sand and grit get up into the layers so you will want to run water on the leek, using your fingers to carefully expose each layer to get it clean.

ANOTHER CHICKEN STOCK RECIPE

Makes approximately 2½ quarts

4 pounds bone-in chicken legs
2 onions, quartered
2–3 carrots, roughly chopped
2–3 celery stalks, roughly chopped
5 garlic cloves, chopped
Salt and pepper to taste
2 bay leaves
1 teaspoon dried thyme
1 teaspoon dried sage
About 2–3 quarts water, to cover

Place ingredients in 8- to 10-quart stockpot. Bring to a boil. Reduce heat and simmer for 2 to 3 hours. Skim off foam that rises to the top. Stir occasionally.

Once stock has cooked, remove from heat and let sit for a few minutes. Remove chicken from stock and set aside. Strain remaining vegetables from stock. Refrigerate stock and let fat congeal on surface. Using a slotted spoon, remove congealed fat. Stock is now ready for immediate use. If not using immediately, refrigerate for up to 4 days or freeze for up to 2 months.

Remove meat from bones, then chop and use in soups, sandwiches, casseroles, or salads.

BEEF STOCK

Makes approximately 2 quarts

4–5 pounds beef soup bones with meat
3–4 large carrots, roughly chopped
2–3 celery stalks, roughly chopped
2 onions, quartered
½ head cabbage, cored and quartered
3–4 sprigs parsley
2 bay leaves
2 garlic cloves, chopped
Salt and pepper to taste
1 teaspoon dried thyme
About 2–3 quarts water, to cover

Preheat oven to 375°F.

Place bones, carrots, celery, and onions in large shallow roasting pan. Bake uncovered for about 1 hour or until bones and vegetables are browned. Stir often and watch them so that they do not blacken or burn.

Transfer bones, vegetables, and drippings to an 8- to 10-quart stockpot. Pour about 1 cup water into warm roasting pan, scrape all the browned bits off the bottom of the pan, and pour this into stockpot.

Add remaining ingredients to stockpot. Cover with water and bring to a boil. Reduce heat and simmer 3 to 4 hours.

Once stock has cooked, remove from heat and let sit for a few minutes. Remove bones from stock. Set bones aside.

Strain remaining vegetables from stock. Refrigerate stock and let fat congeal on surface. Remove congealed fat. Stock is now ready for immediate use. If not using immediately, refrigerate for up to 4 days or freeze for up to 2 months.

Remove meat from bones and use meat in soups, sandwiches, casseroles, or salads.

A Note for Thanksgiving Turkey Carcass Keepers

I positively adore my Carcass Soup. I know that sounds rather macabre—making soup from the skeletal remains of what was once a happy little turkey. It is sort of a scavenger thing to do, like a vulture in the company of roadkill but it takes a certain degree of culinary skill. When I see a turkey carcass, I see good eating straight ahead. Here's what I do to make my world-famous Thanksgiving Carcass Soup.

First, take the carcass apart, throw it in the roaster, and fling some quartered onions, carrots, and celery, and about 8 whole cloves of garlic in there. Then drizzle this mess with some olive oil.

At this point, it is flung in the oven at 425°F for about 45 minutes. The house will smell like Thanksgiving all over again! Let the pan cool for a few minutes, then put the roaster on the stovetop, add cold water (about ¾ of the way up in the pan), and boil the whole thing right there for another hour. Next, strain it and put the broth in the fridge overnight.

The next morning, take off the top layer of fat. You now have this incredibly wonderful broth, ready for Turkey Noodle Soup (using those big thick noodles). Here is my easy soup "recipe."

Let's say you have about 3 quarts of broth, okay? Don't worry that you need to measure your lovely broth—nope, you don't need to do that! Just set it aside and follow the recipe.

Makes approximately 4 quarts

2 tablespoons olive oil
3 carrots, chopped

1 large onion, chopped

2 celery stalks, chopped

1 teaspoon dried thyme

½ bay leaf

Salt and pepper to taste (that means you have to taste it to see how salty
  and peppery you want it!)

3 quarts (or so) turkey broth

1 (1-pound) bag extra-wide noodles

In a large soup pot, heat the oil over medium-high heat. Add the carrots, onion, and celery and cook till translucent, about 5 minutes.

Add the thyme, bay leaf, and salt and pepper. Now add the turkey broth and bring to a boil. When the veggies are nearly cooked, add the noodles and cook till noodles are tender, about 5 minutes.

That's all there is to it! It's very, very easy and satisfyingly good.

What is it about chicken soup that is so wonderful? This is the stuff that your mother made for you, the stuff that makes a cold go away and grants instantaneous health—if we all believed our grandmothers.

There is, believe it or not, some science behind the goodness of chicken soup. Seriously! Researchers at the Nebraska Medical Center in Omaha found this out via the kitchen first, not the laboratory. They made a big batch of chicken soup, gathered up some volunteers, collected the neutrophils from their blood (neutrophils are a type of white blood cell important for fighting infection; neutrophils actually seek out germs and kill them), and mixed them with the chicken soup. No eating allowed; this was science in action.

Guess what? The experiment was a success and they found that the soup does help stop inflammation—even when chicken soup is in a test tube! Grandma was right all along: soup is good for whatever ails you.

So if you're feeling puny, as we say in the South, you need your chicken soup. Even if you're not, I think it's important to have a standard-issue soup recipe that can be doctored up or down to fit the mood. Here's a chicken soup recipe that is as good for the soul as it is for whatever ails you.

Serves 12

1 tablespoon olive oil
1 large onion, chopped
4 garlic cloves, pressed
2 large carrots, chopped
2 small celery stalks, chopped
1 turnip, chopped
2 cups sliced green beans, sliced into 1-inch pieces
1/4 head cabbage, chopped
1/2 teaspoon dried thyme
Salt and pepper to taste
2 small russet potatoes, peeled and chopped
2 cans diced tomatoes, undrained
6 cups chicken broth

In a large soup pot, heat the olive oil over medium-high heat. Add the onion and cook till nearly translucent about 4 to 6 minutes. Now add the garlic. Don't let the garlic brown, but sauté another couple of minutes.

Add the rest of the chopped veggies and green beans, except for the potatoes and tomatoes, sautéing for just a minute or two. You're not cooking them—just sautéing for the wonderful flavor this quick step will add to your soup. Add the thyme and salt and pepper while sautéing.

Now put the veggies in the slow-cooker. Add the potatoes, tomatoes, and broth. Cook on low for 7 to 9 hours (depending on your cooker) or high for 4 to 6 hours. (All slow-cookers are different, depending on size, age, brand, etc.) Just before serving, gently mash some of the potato chunks against the side of the pot to thicken the soup, give it a stir, and serve.

PER SERVING:
88 Calories; 4g Total Fat; 5g Protein; 2g Dietary Fiber; 9g Carbohydrate; 0mg Cholesterol; 658mg Sodium. Food Exchanges: 0 Grain (Starch); 1/2 Lean Meat; 1 Vegetable; 0 Fruit; 1/2 Fat; 0 Other Carbohydrates.

SERVING SUGGESTIONS: Grilled cheese sandwiches on whole-grain bread and a spinach salad.

QUICK FIXES FOR VARIATIONS ON THE
BASIC CHICKEN SOUP

Now remember, don't do this to the whole pot of soup! Just the little bit you pull out to fix yourself for lunch.

QUICK FIX 1—TEX-MEX VEGGIE SOUP. Add some (eyeball it—how much do you want?) drained and rinsed canned black beans, a little bit of cumin, and some chopped cilantro. Top with some tortilla chips and cheese or serve with a quesadilla.

QUICK FIX 2—TUSCAN VEGGIE SOUP. Add some (eyeball it again) drained and rinsed canned cannellini (white kidney beans) or white beans, a little bit of Italian seasoning, and some chopped kale. Cook till heated through and the kale is tender, about 6 to 8 minutes.

QUICK FIX 3—MINESTRONE VEGGIE SOUP. Add some cooked pasta, a little dried basil, and a topping of freshly grated Parmesan cheese.

QUICK FIX 4—AUTUMN VEGGIE SOUP. Add some diced acorn squash or butternut squash, some cooked brown rice, a sprinkling of nutmeg, and some chopped parsley. Cook till heated through and squash is cooked, about 6 to 8 minutes.

At this point, you're going to need some more soup recipes. You have the stock recipes, now you need to make soup. Here are some fabulous and easy soup recipes that you're just going to be so proud to serve your family. Check them out.

CREAM OF ONION SOUP

Serves 4–6

¼ cup (½ stick) butter
2½ large onions, finely diced
1 garlic clove, pressed
5 tablespoons flour
Salt and pepper to taste
3 cups beef broth
3 cups half-and-half
Worcestershire sauce

In a large saucepan over medium-low heat, melt butter and sauté onions. Cook slowly until tender and translucent, about 10 minutes. Add garlic and sauté another 5 minutes.

Add flour, salt, pepper, and broth. Whisk well to incorporate and allow soup to come to a boil, then reduce heat and simmer for about 15 minutes to thicken.

Add half-and-half and simmer for about 10 minutes more. Season with Worcestershire sauce to taste. Ladle into bowls and serve.

PER SERVING:
355 Calories; 31g Fat; 5g Protein; 14g Carbohydrate; 1g Dietary Fiber; 100mg Cholesterol; 189mg Sodium. Exchanges: 1/2 Grain (Starch); 1/2 Vegetable; 6 Fat; 1/2 Other Carbohydrates.

SMOKY PUMPKIN SOUP

Serves 4–6

1 onion, diced

2 celery stalks, diced

2 carrots, diced

3 tablespoons vegetable oil

1 (15-ounce) can pumpkin purée (the can could say just 100%
pumpkin—same thing)

4 cups chicken broth

½ teaspoon ground cumin

½ teaspoon ground cinnamon

⅛ teaspoon ground nutmeg

1 cup heavy cream

Grated Gouda cheese (optional)

In a large saucepan or stockpot, sauté onion, celery, and carrots in oil over medium-low heat till vegetables are translucent and tender, not browned, about 4 to 6 minutes.

Add pumpkin, broth, cumin, cinnamon, and nutmeg to saucepan stockpot. Stir well to incorporate ingredients. Bring to a boil. Reduce heat and simmer for 15 to 20 minutes.

Remove from heat and stir in cream. Sprinkle on cheese, if desired, and serve.

PER SERVING:
253 Calories; 20g Fat; 7g Protein; 13g Carbohydrate; 3g Dietary Fiber; 43mg Cholesterol; 606mg Sodium. Exchanges: 0 Grain (Starch); 1/2 Lean Meat; 2 Vegetable; 3 1/2 Fat; 0 Other Carbohydrates.

POTATO SAUSAGE SOUP

Serves 4–6

> 1 onion, chopped
> 2 garlic cloves, pressed
> 2 celery stalks, chopped
> 3 tablespoons olive oil
> 5 cups chicken broth
> 2 cups cored and finely chopped cabbage
> 4 potatoes, sliced
> 1 carrot, sliced
> 1 pound kielbasa, sliced
> Salt and pepper
> Grated Parmesan cheese

In a large saucepan or stockpot, sauté onion, garlic, and celery in oil over medium heat until onion is translucent, about 4 to 6 minutes.

Add broth, cabbage, potatoes, and carrot. Bring to a boil, reduce heat, and simmer about 15 minutes or until carrots and potatoes are just about tender.

Add kielbasa to soup, cover, and simmer another 5 to 7 minutes or until sausage is warmed through. Add salt and pepper to taste. Serve garnished with Parmesan cheese, if desired.

PER SERVING:
446 Calories; 29g Fat; 24g Protein; 23g Carbohydrate; 3g Dietary Fiber; 55mg Cholesterol; 1366mg Sodium. Exchanges: 1 Grain (Starch); 3 Lean Meat; 1 Vegetable; 4 1/2 Fat.

LONDON FOG SPLIT PEA SOUP

Serves 4–6

2 cups split peas, rinsed and picked over
2 tablespoons olive oil
1 onion, chopped
2 carrots, diced
1 large celery stalk and top, chopped
1 teaspoon dried thyme
10 cups water
Salt and pepper
1 ham hock or 1 smoked turkey leg

Place cleaned split peas in a slow-cooker.

In a skillet, heat oil over medium heat. Sauté onion, carrots, and celery for about 3 minutes, then add to slow-cooker. Add thyme. Fill the slow-cooker with the water, add salt and pepper to taste, and bury the ham hock or turkey leg in the peas. Cook on low for 8 to 10 hours. Ladle into bowls and serve.

PER SERVING:
326 Calories; 8g Fat; 20g Protein; 44g Carbohydrate; 18g Dietary Fiber; 18mg Cholesterol; 29mg Sodium. Exchanges: 2 1/2 Grain (Starch); 1 1/2 Lean Meat; 1 Vegetable; 1 Fat.

ROASTED VEGETABLE
CHEDDAR SOUP

Serves 4–6

2 large rutabagas, peeled and quartered
2 large turnips, peeled and quartered
1 large onion, quartered
6 garlic cloves
1 large head of cauliflower, broken up into florets
3 tablespoons olive oil
Salt and pepper to taste
1½ teaspoons dried thyme
3 cups chicken or vegetable broth
1½ cups grated low-fat cheddar cheese
1 tablespoon flour
1½ cups half-and-half

Preheat oven to 425°F.

In a large roasting pan, place all the vegetables and toss well with the olive oil, salt and pepper, and thyme. Cook for 30 minutes or until veggies start to turn brown. Remove from the oven, set aside, and let cool.

In a blender, combine cooled roasted veggies and ¼ cup of the broth (no more—you just want to help the blender blend the veggies and it needs liquid). Pulse the blender—you don't want your veggies liquefied, just blended. In the meantime, put the cheese in a bowl, add the flour, and toss to coat the cheese.

Dump the contents of the blender in a large saucepan, add the rest of the broth, and heat to boiling. Lower the heat to a simmer and add the half-and-half. When hot (but *not* boiling, or the half-and-half will separate!), add the cheese tossed with the flour. Again, bring to almost boiling, turn down the heat, simmer for 2 to 3 minutes, then serve.

PER SERVING:
345 Calories; 17g Total Fat; 13g Protein; 3g Dietary Fiber; 14g Carbohydrate; 111mg Cholesterol; 616mg Sodium. Food Exchanges: 0 Grain (Starch); 1 Lean Meat; 1 Vegetable; 0 Fruit; 7 Fat; 0 Other Carbohydrates.

CHICKEN, VEGETABLE, AND BEAN SOUP

Serves 6

1 cup dried great northern beans

6 cups water

1 large onion, chopped

1 small fennel bulb, trimmed and sliced into ½-inch pieces (optional, if you can't find it or don't like fennel, that's fine!)

2 carrots, chopped

2 garlic cloves, pressed

2 tablespoons chopped parsley

1 teaspoon dried thyme

1 teaspoon dried marjoram

Salt and pepper

4 boneless skinless chicken breast halves, chopped into 1-inch pieces (Hint: Partially thaw frozen chicken breast halves for ease in cutting)

5 cups low-sodium chicken broth

1 (14.5-ounce) can diced tomatoes (undrained)

Soak dried beans overnight in the 6 cups water. Drain and rinse beans.

In a slow-cooker, place onion, fennel, carrots, garlic, parsley, thyme, marjoram, and salt and pepper to taste. Place beans and chicken on top of veggies; cover with chicken broth. Cover slow-cooker and cook on low for 8 to 10 hours or on high for 4 to 5 hours. During last 30 minutes of cooking time, turn temperature to high or leave on high and pour in diced tomatoes. Cover and let cook the last 30 minutes, then serve.

PER SERVING:
277 Calories; 2g Fat; 36g Protein; 31g Carbohydrate; 9g Dietary Fiber; 46mg Cholesterol; 532mg Sodium. Exchanges: 1 1/2 Grain (Starch); 4 Lean Meat; 1 1/2 Vegetable; 0 Fat.

ESAU'S POTTAGE

Serves 4–6

1¾ *cups dried lentils, rinsed*
1 *large sweet potato, peeled and cut into 1-inch chunks*
1 *(28-ounce) jar spaghetti sauce (your favorite)*
2 *cups green beans, cut in half*
1 *small bell pepper, diced*
1 *large potato, diced*
1 *onion, chopped*
2 *garlic cloves, pressed*

In a slow-cooker, mix all ingredients and add 3 cups water.

Cover and cook on low for 8 to 10 hours or until the vegetables and lentils are tender. Serve.

PER SERVING:
403 Calories; 3g Fat; 21g Protein; 81g Carbohydrate; 26g Dietary Fiber; 0mg Cholesterol; 227mg Sodium. Exchanges: 4 1/2 Grain (Starch); 1 1/2 Lean Meat; 2 1/2 Vegetable; 1/2 Fat.

SWEET MINESTRONE SOUP

Serves 4–6

1 tablespoon olive oil

1 cup diced onion

¾ cup thinly sliced celery

1 cup diced carrot

½ pound smoked turkey sausage, cut into ¼-inch slices

3 cups low-sodium chicken broth

2 cups diced peeled sweet potato

1 teaspoon dried oregano

Salt and pepper to taste

1 (28-ounce) can whole tomatoes, undrained, coarsely chopped

1 (15-ounce) can cannellini beans or other white beans, rinsed and
drained

8 cups coarsely chopped fresh spinach

In a soup pot, heat olive oil over medium-high heat; add onion, celery, and carrot and sauté till onion is translucent. Now add sausage and continue to cook until sausage is browned, about 5 minutes.

Add chicken broth, sweet potatoes, oregano, salt and pepper, tomatoes, and beans. Bring to a boil, cover, reduce heat, and simmer 20 to 30 minutes or until vegetables are tender. Stir in spinach; cook for just a minute and serve hot.

PER SERVING:
275 Calories; 10g Total Fat; 15g Protein; 39g Carbohydrate; 30mg Cholesterol; 422mg Sodium. Exchanges: 1 1/2 Grain (Starch); 1 Lean Meat; 2 1/2 Vegetable; 0 Fruit; 1 Fat; 0 Other Carbohydrates.

Serves 4–6

4–6 onions, cut into thick slices (use Sweet Vidalia if you can find them)

2 tablespoons olive oil

4–6 cups low-sodium beef broth

1 teaspoon dried thyme

Salt and pepper

4–6 tablespoons dry sherry, or grape juice with a splash of vinegar

4–6 slices toasted French bread

4–6 slices provolone cheese

Preheat oven to 350°F.

In a large soup pot, over medium-high heat, sauté onions in olive oil for about 10 minutes, until soft and browning nicely. Add broth, thyme, salt and pepper to taste, and sherry; simmer for 15 minutes.

Ladle soup into ovenproof bowls. Place bowls on a cookie sheet in oven. Top each bowl with a slice of toast and a slice of cheese on top of the toast.

Bake for 13 to 14 minutes or until the cheese is melted. Serve at once.

PER SERVING:
330 Calories; 13g Fat; 22g Protein; 28g Carbohydrate; 3g Dietary Fiber; 20mg Cholesterol; 1684mg Sodium. Exchanges: 1 Grain (Starch); 2 Lean Meat; 1 1/2 Vegetable; 2 Fat.

SPEEDY TACO SOUP

Serves 4–6

1 (11-ounce) can Mexican-style corn kernels
1 (16-ounce) can chili beans in zesty sauce
2 (14.5-ounce) cans low-sodium chicken broth
1 (16-ounce) jar salsa (your favorite)
2½ cups diced cooked chicken breast
Salt and pepper
¼ cup chopped fresh cilantro
½ cup low-fat sour cream

In a large soup pot over medium heat, combine corn, beans, broth, and salsa. Bring to a boil, then reduce heat to simmer and stir in chicken. Season to taste with salt and pepper and cover. Cook for an additional 5 minutes or until hot. Stir in cilantro, then top with a dollop of sour cream.

PER SERVING:
214 Calories; 8g Fat; 28g Protein; 7g Carbohydrate; 1g Dietary Fiber; 71mg Cholesterol; 546mg Sodium. Exchanges: 0 Grain (Starch); 3 1/2 Lean Meat; 1/2 Vegetable; 0 Fat; 0 Other Carbohydrates.

SUMMER GAZPACHO

Serves 4–6

1½ cups chopped celery

¾ bunch parsley, chopped

¼ cup balsamic vinegar

1 (32-ounce) bottle or can low-sodium V-8 juice

1½ cups chopped ripe tomatoes

4 garlic cloves, pressed

1½ cups de-ribbed, seeded, and chopped green bell pepper

1 medium cucumber, chopped

1½ cups low-sodium chicken broth

Salt and pepper to taste

Juice of 2 lemons

1½ pounds crabmeat (fresh, frozen, or canned)

Mix all ingredients (except crabmeat) in a bowl, then gently fold in crabmeat. Chill well before serving.

PER SERVING:
200 Calories; 2g Fat; 29g Protein; 11g Carbohydrate; 4g Dietary Fiber; 101mg Cholesterol; 579mg Sodium. Exchanges: 3 1/2 Lean Meat; 3 Vegetable; 0 Fruit.

PASTA AND BEAN SOUP

Serves 6–8

6 slices turkey bacon, diced
1 small onion, finely chopped
1 celery stalk, finely chopped
1 carrot, peeled and grated
2 garlic cloves, pressed
⅛ teaspoon red pepper flakes
2 (8-ounce) cans crushed tomatoes
2½ cups drained canned white beans
6 cups low-sodium chicken broth
¾ cup macaroni or other small pasta (uncooked)
Freshly grated Parmesan cheese (optional)

In a large soup pot, sauté diced bacon until some of the fat is rendered, about 5 minutes. Add onion, celery, carrot, garlic, and red pepper flakes and sauté until vegetables are softened, about 10 minutes. Stir in tomatoes and cook, stirring occasionally, for 10 more minutes.

Stir in beans; add broth and bring to a gentle boil. Add macaroni or other pasta and continue cooking until pasta is al dente, about 5 minutes or so. Serve immediately with Parmesan cheese sprinkled over the top.

PER SERVING:
217 Calories; 4g Fat; 14g Protein; 32g Carbohydrate; 6g Dietary Fiber; 4mg Cholesterol; 741mg Sodium. Exchanges: 1 1/2 Grain (Starch); 1 Lean Meat; 1 1/2 Vegetable; 1/2 Fat.

PASTA CLAM AND VEGETABLE CHOWDER

Serves 6

2 cups small shells, elbow macaroni, or other small pasta (uncooked)
3 cups milk
2 cups low-sodium chicken broth
3 cups chopped fresh vegetables (such as zucchini, yellow squash, carrots)
1 teaspoon dried thyme
1 teaspoon paprika
3 tablespoons cornstarch
2 (6-ounce) cans chopped clams, drained
Salt and pepper

Prepare pasta according to package directions; drain. Rinse pasta under cold water until cool. Drain again.

Combine pasta, 2½ cups milk with chicken broth, vegetables, thyme, and paprika in a 2-quart saucepan. Cook over medium heat until simmering lightly, but don't boil or the milk will separate.

In a separate bowl, stir the remaining ½ cup milk and cornstarch together until cornstarch dissolves. Stir the cornstarch mixture into soup and heat to simmering. Add clams and simmer, stirring frequently, 3 minutes. Add salt and pepper to taste. Serve hot.

PER SERVING:
270 Calories; 2g Fat; 21g Protein; 41g Carbohydrate; 3g Dietary Fiber; 38mg Cholesterol; 95mg Sodium. Exchanges: 2 Grain (Starch); 2 Lean Meat; 1 1/2 Vegetable; 0 Fat; 0 Other Carbohydrates.

SALADS

All right, so I have a second pet peeve. That would be iceberg lettuce. Honestly, I have no idea why this lettuce exists in the first place. It's 97 percent water, completely bereft nutritionally; licking an envelope is more flavorful than this sad sack of salad.

The antidote to lackluster salad is exchanging the bad stuff for the good stuff. And while it's always best and less expensive to buy heads of fresh lettuce, I never do anymore. I have found that if you're careful and selective, you can get fabulous, already washed, and ready-to-go lettuces in a wide assortment of flavors, types, and styles. You can mix, match, and pair these lettuces with already shredded carrots, cabbage, and whatever else you find in the produce department willing to take home with you. Add a generous sprinkling of crumbled feta cheese, some pine nuts, a splash of olive oil, fresh pepper, and a touch of balsamic vinegar, and you have a cover girl of a salad that took all of three minutes to slap together.

There are also main-course salads that will save your soul from wilting during the dog days of August, and there are some good ones right here ready for you to take them on. Just keep in mind that a salad side dish should never take more time to prepare than the meal. When it's the main course, well—that's different. Here are some favorite main-course salads that everyone will love.

STEAK SALAD WITH
CREAMY RANCH DRESSING

Serves 4–6

2 garlic cloves, pressed
¾ teaspoon brown sugar
¾ teaspoon cayenne pepper
1 tablespoon olive oil
Salt and pepper to taste
1 (1½-pound) ¾-inch-thick sirloin steak
1 (16-ounce) bag washed spinach
3 cups cherry tomatoes
1 large red onion, sliced
1 large cucumber, peeled, seeded, and sliced
Ranch dressing (your choice)
Croutons (optional)

Preheat an outdoor or indoor grill or oven broiler.

Combine garlic, brown sugar, cayenne pepper, oil, salt, and pepper. Rub this mixture over both sides of steak. Grill steak until it reaches desired level of doneness, anywhere from 4 to 8 mintues per side depending on how you like it. Remove steak from grill and let it sit for about 5 minutes to let juices set. Keep warm. While steak sits, prep salad.

Combine spinach, tomatoes, onion, and cucumber in a large bowl. Slice steak diagonally across the grain. Top salad with steak. Toss. Add ranch dressing and croutons. Serve.

PER SERVING:
379 Calories; 26g Fat; 25g Protein; 12g Carbohydrate; 4g Dietary Fiber; 74mg Cholesterol; 294mg Sodium. Exchanges: 0 Grain (Starch); 3 Lean Meat; 2 Vegetable; 3 1/2 Fat; 0 Other Carbohydrates.

ASIAN CHICKEN SALAD

Serves 4–6

¾ cup Asian-style salad dressing

¼ cup chopped fresh cilantro

2 tablespoons grated fresh ginger

1 (10-ounce) bag washed spinach

1 small red bell pepper, de-ribbed, seeded, and chopped

3 cups chopped, cooked chicken thigh meat

½ cup honey-roasted peanuts

Salt and pepper to taste

1 mango, peeled and sliced

Combine salad dressing, cilantro, and ginger in a small bowl.

Toss spinach, bell pepper, chicken, and peanuts in a large bowl with enough dressing mixture to coat evenly. Season to taste with salt and pepper and divide evenly among six dinner plates. Top with mango and serve.

PER SERVING:
278 Calories; 11g Fat; 32g Protein; 14g Carbohydrate; 3g Dietary Fiber; 69mg Cholesterol; 150mg Sodium. Exchanges: 1/2 Grain (Starch); 4 Lean Meat; 0 Vegetable; 1/2 Fruit; 1 1/2 Fat; 0 Other Carbohydrates.

Grating Ginger Gingerly

Dealing with fresh ginger can be somewhat of a pain. After you pick up that alien-looking root mass at the grocery store, you might be somewhat unsure about what to do with it.

There are several options, actually. The first is to peel the thin skin off the ginger using a paring knife and discard the peel, then using a grater (small holes), you grate away. That makes a mess and wastes a lot of ginger. Another option is to use your trusty garlic press. All you have to do is put a garlic clove–size hunk in the press and squeeze away. It's easy, you don't have to peel the ginger and you waste a whole lot less.

LAYERED SUMMER SALAD

Serves 4–6

1 (16-ounce) package mixed baby greens
1 red bell pepper, de-ribbed, seeded, and thinly sliced
3 green onions, finely chopped
1 cup chopped cauliflower florets
1 cup thinly sliced celery
3 large tomatoes, sliced
1 cup chopped broccoli florets
4 hard-boiled eggs, chopped
8 ounces snow peas, trimmed
2 carrots, shredded
½ head small cabbage, cored and shredded
Salad dressing (your choice)
Grated low-fat cheddar cheese

In a large salad bowl or deep-dish casserole, layer vegetables in order listed. Cover with salad dressing and sprinkle on cheese.

Refrigerate for 2 hours, then serve. (Note: you can serve it without the long chilling time.)

PER SERVING:
341 Calories; 25g Fat; 12g Protein; 20g Carbohydrate; 7g Dietary Fiber; 133mg Cholesterol; 590mg Sodium. Exchanges: 1 Lean Meat; 3 Vegetable; 4 1/2 Fat; 0 Other Carbohydrates.

ITALIAN CHEF SALAD

Serves 4–6

8 cups romaine lettuce, in bite-size pieces
1 pound white mushrooms, sliced
8 ounces sliced smoked turkey, cut into strips
4 ounces sliced provolone cheese, cut into strips (about 1 cup)
1 medium tomato, cut into 8 wedges
½ cup red onion, sliced into rings
½ cup Italian salad dressing

In a large salad bowl, place lettuce, mushrooms, turkey, cheese, tomato, and red onion. Add dressing; toss well and serve on individual plates.

PER SERVING:

204 Calories; 9g Fat; 22g Protein; 13g Carbohydrate; 7g Dietary Fiber; 39mg Cholesterol; 218mg Sodium. Exchanges: 2 Lean Meat; 2 1/2 Vegetable; 1/2 Fat.

PASTA CHOPPED SALAD

Serves 6–8

¼ cup Dijon mustard
2 tablespoons olive oil
¼ cup balsamic vinegar
1 pound small shells or other small pasta
4 ounces cooked turkey ham, diced into ¼-inch cubes
½ cup diced Swiss cheese, diced into ¼-inch cubes
2 celery stalks, chopped
3 green onions, sliced
½ cup diced red onion
¼ cup diced pitted black olives
Salt and freshly ground pepper

In a small bowl, whisk the mustard, olive oil, and vinegar until blended. Set aside.

In the meantime, prepare pasta according to package directions; drain, add dressing to the pasta and toss. Doing it warm this way will help the pasta become more flavorful with less refrigeration.

Place the pasta mixture, turkey ham, cheese, celery, green onions, red onion, and olives in a mixing bowl. Season with salt and pepper to taste.

Refrigerate for 2 hours, then serve. (Note: you can serve it without the long chilling time.)

PER SERVING:

305 Calories; 8g Fat; 13g Protein; 46g Carbohydrate; 2g Dietary Fiber; 14mg Cholesterol; 309mg Sodium. Exchanges: 3 Grain (Starch); 1/2 Lean Meat; 1/2 Vegetable; 0 Fruit; 1 Fat; 0 Other Carbohydrates.

ISLAND SALAD

6 cups torn romaine lettuce

1½ pounds medium shrimp, cooked and peeled (optional)

1½ cups cubed peeled papaya

1½ cups cubed fresh pineapple (or use canned)

¾ cup chopped peeled avocado (see below for instructions on cutting avocado)

¾ cup de-ribbed, seeded, and chopped red bell pepper

1 (15-ounce) can black beans, rinsed and drained

¾ cup shredded reduced-fat Monterey Jack cheese

1 cup Asian-style salad dressing

¼ cup chopped toasted unsalted cashews

Toss first 8 ingredients together gently in a large mixing bowl. Add dressing and toss very gently again; garnish with cashews and serve.

PER SERVING:
327 Calories; 10g Fat; 33g Protein; 26g Carbohydrate; 7g Dietary Fiber; 177mg Cholesterol; 472mg Sodium. Exchanges: 1/2 Grain (Starch); 4 Lean Meat; 1/2 Vegetable; 1/2 Fruit; 1 Fat; 0 Other Carbohydrates.

Using a paring knife, carefully slice the avocado in half lengthwise.

After cutting the avocado, pry it open using your hands.

Stick the knife blade into the slippery pit to remove it easily. Simply pull your knife out once it is lodged into the pit, and the pit will stay on the knife and come out.

SUMMER PASTA SALAD

1 (16-ounce) package bow-tie pasta, cooked and drained
1 (12-ounce) jar marinated artichoke hearts, drained and sliced
1 (7-ounce) jar roasted red peppers, drained and sliced
1 (2¼-ounce) can sliced ripe olives, drained
2 tablespoons capers, drained
1 cup diced provolone cheese
2 cups diced tomatoes
Salt and pepper to taste
⅓ cup olive oil
3 tablespoons balsamic vinegar
2 tablespoons chopped fresh basil leaves

In a large bowl, combine first 7 ingredients. Add salt and pepper, oil, and vinegar and toss. Add basil and toss again. Chill for 2 hours, then serve.

PER SERVING:
403 Calories; 17g Fat; 13g Protein; 48g Carbohydrate; 4g Dietary Fiber; 11mg Cholesterol; 375mg Sodium. Exchanges: 3 Grain (Starch); 1/2 Lean Meat; 1 Vegetable; 0 Fruit; 3 Fat; 0 Other Carbohydrates.

Serves 6

6 cups cooked brown rice
⅓ cup apple cider vinegar
½ cup creamy-style peanut butter
4 tablespoons water
4 tablespoons soy sauce, low sodium if available
1 tablespoon hoisin sauce (in the Asian section of grocery store)
Salt to taste
3 cups shredded carrots
3 cups sliced bok choy
1½ cups chopped green onions
¾ cup chopped fresh cilantro
18 ounces extra-firm tofu, cubed

Set rice aside and allow it to cool to room temperature.

Place vinegar, peanut butter, water, soy sauce, hoisin sauce, and salt in a bowl. Whisk till well blended.

Place rice in a large serving bowl and add carrots, bok choy, green onions, cilantro, and tofu. Toss to combine. Drizzle dressing over salad and serve.

PER SERVING:
474 Calories; 17g Fat; 20g Protein; 66g Carbohydrate; 8g Dietary Fiber; trace Cholesterol; 609mg Sodium. Exchanges: 3 1/2 Grain (Starch); 2 1/2 Lean Meat; 2 Vegetable; 2 Fat; 0 Other Carbohydrates.

CHICKEN SPINACH SALAD

Serves 4–6

1½ pounds boneless skinless chicken tenders
1⅛ cups honey-mustard barbecue sauce
1⅛ cups water
2 (10-ounce) bags torn fresh spinach
1½ cups slivered red onion
1 (15-ounce) can mandarin orange sections

Stir together the chicken tenders and barbecue sauce in medium bowl. Let stand 5 minutes.

Heat a large nonstick skillet over medium-high heat. Add chicken and sauce; stir-fry until chicken is no longer pink, about 6 minutes. Add water and bring to a simmer.

Arrange spinach, onion, and oranges on six individual plates. Top with chicken and sauce. Serve immediately.

PER SERVING:
185 Calories; 2g Fat; 29g Protein; 11g Carbohydrate; 2g Dietary Fiber; 70mg Cholesterol; 448mg Sodium. Exchanges: 3 1/2 Lean Meat; 1/2 Vegetable; 0 Fruit; 1/2 Other Carbohydrates.

CHICKEN DIJON SALAD

Serves 4–6

1 pound red potatoes, quartered
1 cup sliced fresh green beans
1½ tablespoons olive oil
2¼ tablespoons wine vinegar
¾ cup honey mustard
¾ tablespoon Dijon mustard
1½ tablespoons minced fresh parsley
Salt and pepper
1½ cups cubed cooked chicken
1 small red bell pepper, de-ribbed, seeded, and diced

In a large saucepan, boil potatoes until tender, about 20 minutes. Drain and set aside.

Briefly cook green beans in boiling water, about 2 minutes. Drain and rinse under cold water. Set aside.

Combine oil, vinegar, mustards, parsley, and salt and pepper to taste. Mix thoroughly.

Place potatoes, green beans, chicken, and red bell pepper in a large bowl. Add dressing; toss to coat well. Chill for 2 hours, then serve.

PER SERVING:
177 Calories; 5g Fat; 13g Protein; 20g Carbohydrate; 3g Dietary Fiber; 30mg Cholesterol; 162mg Sodium. Exchanges: 1 Grain (Starch); 1 1/2 Lean Meat; 1/2 Vegetable; 1/2 Fat; 0 Other Carbohydrates.

SALMON GARDEN SALAD

1 small red onion, thinly sliced

3 ripe tomatoes, seeded and diced

1 small red bell pepper, de-ribbed, seeded, and diced

6 cups assorted salad greens

½ cup shredded fresh basil

1 carrot, peeled and shredded

1 celery stalk, chopped

½ cup low-calorie Italian salad dressing

4 tablespoons Dijon mustard

1–2 teaspoons balsamic vinegar

1 (14.75-ounce) can Alaskan salmon, drained and flaked (or same amount fresh)

Salt and pepper

¾ cup shredded mozzarella cheese

In a large bowl, combine onion, tomatoes, red bell pepper, salad greens, basil, carrot, and celery. Mix well.

In a separate bowl, mix the salad dressing, mustard, and vinegar. Add the dressing mixture and the salmon to the salad greens and combine thoroughly, salt and pepper to taste. Portion evenly onto chilled dinner plates; top with cheese and serve.

PER SERVING:
139 Calories; 4g Fat; 16g Protein; 11g Carbohydrate; 3g Dietary Fiber; 31mg Cholesterol; 700mg Sodium. Exchanges: 1 1/2 Lean Meat; 1 1/2 Vegetable; 0 Fruit; 0 Fat; 0 Other Carbohydrates.

TURKEY CITRUS SALAD WITH POPPY SEED DRESSING

Serves 6

9 cups washed spinach leaves
4½ cups fresh grapefruit sections, drained, juice reserved
3 cups orange sections, drained, juice reserved
3 cups cubed cooked turkey
1½ teaspoons honey
¾ teaspoon dry mustard
¾ teaspoon paprika
⅓ teaspoon garlic powder
¾ teaspoon poppy seeds
Dash of ground ginger
⅓ cup low-fat mayonnaise

Arrange spinach leaves on six salad plates. Arrange grapefruit and orange sections alternately in spoke-wheel fashion on spinach.

Place ½ cup turkey in center of each fruit wheel.

In a small bowl, measure ¼ cup reserved orange juice, adding grapefruit juice to equal ½ cup. Add remaining ingredients and mix thoroughly. Pour over the top of the salads and serve.

PER SERVING:
271 Calories; 8g Fat; 24g Protein; 29g Carbohydrate; 5g Dietary Fiber; 58mg Cholesterol; 148mg Sodium. Exchanges: 0 Grain (Starch); 3 Lean Meat; 1/2 Vegetable; 1 1/2 Fruit; 1 Fat; 0 Other Carbohydrates.

POTATO SALAD WITH SALMON

Serves 6

1½ cups low-fat mayonnaise

¼ cup chopped fresh cilantro, plus additional for garnish

1 garlic clove, pressed

⅓ cup diced red onion

1 celery stalk, diced

1 (4¾-ounce) can salmon, drained and flaked (or same amount fresh)

2½ pounds red potatoes, cooked and quartered

Salt and pepper to taste

12 cups fresh spinach leaves

In a large bowl, combine mayonnaise, cilantro, garlic, onion, and celery. Add salmon and potatoes; gently mix all ingredients to coat with dressing. Taste, adding salt and pepper as necessary. If possible, chill for 1 to 3 hours. Serve salad on a bed of fresh spinach. Garnish with additional chopped cilantro.

PER SERVING:
424 Calories; 21g Fat; 20g Protein; 41g Carbohydrate; 5g Dietary Fiber; 58mg Cholesterol; 734mg Sodium. Exchanges: 2 Grain (Starch); 1 1/2 Lean Meat; 1/2 Vegetable; 3 Fat; 1/2 Other Carbohydrates.

LEMON BLUEBERRY CHICKEN SALAD

Serves 4–6

1 cup low-fat lemon yogurt

4 tablespoons low-fat mayonnaise

1 teaspoon salt

3 cups fresh or frozen blueberries

3 cups cubed cooked chicken breast

¾ cup sliced green onions

¾ cup diagonally sliced celery

¾ cup de-ribbed, seeded, and diced red bell pepper

9 cups mixed greens (I love butter lettuce and romaine for this)

In a medium bowl, combine yogurt, mayonnaise, and salt. Add blueberries, chicken, green onions, celery, and bell pepper; mix gently. Cover and refrigerate to let flavors blend, at least 30 minutes.

Serve salad on top of mixed greens.

PER SERVING:
308 Calories; 11g Fat; 32g Protein; 20g Carbohydrate; 3g Dietary Fiber; 86mg Cholesterol; 708mg Sodium. Exchanges: 4 Lean Meat; 1/2 Vegetable; 1/2 Fruit; 1/2 Fat; 1/2 Other Carbohydrates.

CHAPTER TEN

ONE-STEP DINNERS

Without a doubt, one of the toughest challenges for most people is getting dinner on the table, night after night, when the time crunch is on. Even if you're single, the fact is, you don't have hefty amounts of time to devote to the art of cooking when your tummy is telling you it's hungry. At that time of the afternoon or early evening, you're necessarily all about easy, simple, and getting it done. What you want is a big return on a small investment. And since that most likely isn't going to be happening anytime soon in the stock market, how about doing it with dinner? That alone is a good enough reason to invest some hard-earned capital in a good skillet and slow-cooker. Dinner can nearly pop right out of both of these hardworking dinner tools.

Another favorite, which was mentioned earlier in the equipment chapter (page 11), is the wok. This creature can make a mountain of stir-fry in a heartbeat. The thing to understand about wok cooking is that it's a pan that necessitates a technique—that's all. You don't have to go Asian to use your wok.

I make my fajitas in the wok and anything else stir-fried, including chicken, other meats, fish, and vegetables done in a variety of ways.

And sometimes I go naked—no recipe! When I make sautéed vegetables (especially if there is more than just family here), I inevitably pull out the wok to get my sauté on. Woks are merely sauté pans with higher sloping sides than skillets. Those sides help you keep the food moving easily (with less accidental overboards), and they handle an impressive volume as well.

Another one step dinner–making instrument is the beloved slow-cooker (aka Crock-Pot, crock cooker, or whatever else you want to call your slow-cooking appliance). This is undoubtedly one of my favorite kitchen tools. Though slow-cookers may seem like a fool-proof way to get dinner on the table, they do have some idiosyncrasies that you should be aware of. Read the sidebar below before you fire yours up.

Twelve things you should know about your slow-cooker before attempting to use it:

1. All of my slow-cooker recipes are best prepared in a 3.5- to 5-quart cooker.

2. Newer slow-cookers cook hotter and faster than their counterparts from 20 years ago. This is important to remember when timing your meals. If you are using a newer cooker, you may need to slightly increase the moisture content in your recipe, decrease the cooking time, or both. Try the recipe out first before leaving the house for the day with your cooker cooking something. This way, you'll know how to adjust the cooking time, if at all.

3. Cooking times will vary depending on the temperature of the ingredients when they are placed in the cooker. Thawed chicken takes less time to cook than cold, nearly frozen chicken. For the most part, use chicken thighs in the cooker, as they hold up better and dry out less.

4. Most slow-cooker manufacturers recommend that the appliance be at least half but not more than two-thirds full. Consult your instruction booklet to get the most from your machine.

5. To keep dairy products from curdling, add these ingredients during the last half hour to hour of cooking time.

6. Remember that every time you remove the lid from your slow cooker, it loses heat; add another 20 to 30 minutes to your cooking time.

7. Keep the size of your ingredients consistent when chopping for use in a

slow-cooker. If your carrots or potatoes vary too much in size, you'll end up with vegetables that are overcooked and mushy, undercooked and crunchy, or both. Place veggies on the bottom to cook better.

8. Meat does not brown when cooked in a slow-cooker. It is not necessary to brown meat before cooking it in a slow-cooker, but it does improve the look, flavor, and texture immensely. Most of my recipes will have you browning the meat, but you don't need to.

9. The slow-cooker is wonderful for taking a tough piece of meat and making it tender and juicy. Therefore, the leaner the cut of meat, the less time it will take to cook. If you are using a very lean or very tender cut of meat, decrease the cooking time by about an hour.

10. Cooking food at high altitudes requires more time.

11. The crockery liners of slow-cookers are sensitive to sudden or drastic temperature changes. Do not preheat your slow-cooker. Do not add a cold crock liner straight from the refrigerator to a hot slow-cooker casing. If you wish to prep your meal the night before, do not place ingredients in the slow-cooker liner and store in the fridge. Prep and store in a resealable plastic bag or in a covered dish. In the morning, transfer those ingredients to a room-temperature slow-cooker liner.

12. No two slow-cookers are the same. Get to know your own cooker. Read the manual. Make adjustments based on your knowledge of your appliance. Check my recipes against the recipes in your manual. Are the portions approximately the same or much different? Adjust the recipes according to the size of the pot, if necessary. This isn't an exact science, but the food does need to fit inside the cooker!

ONE-STEP RECIPES

When doing dinner in a hurry, you need as few steps as possible. These next recipes will get you in and out of the kitchen before you know it.

DIJON-GLAZED FLANK STEAKS

Serves 4–6

4½ tablespoons Dijon mustard
1 large lime, juiced
Salt and pepper to taste
3 garlic cloves, pressed
4–6 (4–6 ounces each) flank steaks

Preheat broiler. Lightly grease broiler pan.

Combine mustard, lime juice, salt, pepper, and garlic in a mixing bowl.

Place steaks on broiler pan. Spoon half the mustard sauce on the steaks. Broil for 4 to 5 minutes. Turn steaks and coat second side with remaining mustard sauce. Broil for 3 to 4 minutes more, or until steaks reach your preferred level of doneness. Serve.

PER SERVING:
192 Calories; 11g Fat; 20g Protein; 2g Carbohydrate; trace Dietary Fiber; 51mg Cholesterol; 212mg Sodium. Exchanges: 3 Lean Meat; 0 Vegetable; 0 Fruit; 1/2 Fat; 0 Other Carbohydrates.

GINGER HONEY-GLAZED SALMON

Serves 4–6

3 teaspoons olive oil
1 tablespoon honey
1 tablespoon Dijon mustard
2 teaspoons grated fresh ginger
4–6 (4–6 ounces each) salmon fillets

Preheat oven to 350°F.

In a small bowl, blend olive oil, honey, mustard, and ginger.

Brush salmon evenly with ginger mixture and place in a medium baking dish. Bake for 15 to 20 minutes, until fish flakes with a fork and is fully cooked but not overcooked. Serve.

PER SERVING:
230 Calories; 8g Fat; 34g Protein; 3g Carbohydrate; trace Dietary Fiber; 88mg Cholesterol; 145mg Sodium. Exchanges: 5 Lean Meat; 0 Vegetable; 1/2 Fat; 0 Other Carbohydrates.

RASPBERRY BALSAMIC-GLAZED CHICKEN

Serves 4–6

1 ½ teaspoons olive oil
¾ cup chopped red onion
¾ teaspoon dried thyme
Salt and pepper to taste
4–6 (4–6 ounces each) skinless boneless chicken breast halves
½ cup all-berry raspberry conserve
3 tablespoons balsamic vinegar

Heat olive oil in a large nonstick skillet over high heat. Add onion and sauté for 3 minutes.

Meanwhile, sprinkle thyme, salt, and pepper on chicken. Add chicken to the skillet and sauté for 6 minutes on each side, or until done. Remove chicken from skillet and keep warm.

Reduce heat to medium-low. Add a little salt, conserve, vinegar, and pepper, stirring constantly until the conserve melts. Spoon sauce over chicken and serve.

PER SERVING:
214 Calories; 3g Fat; 28g Protein; 20g Carbohydrate; 1g Dietary Fiber; 68mg Cholesterol; 88mg Sodium. Exchanges: 0 Grain (Starch); 4 Lean Meat; 1/2 Vegetable; 0 Fruit; 0 Fat; 1 Other Carbohydrates.

DOUBLE-MUSTARD SKILLET
PORK CHOPS

Serves 4–6

4–6 (4–6 ounces each) boneless pork chops
3 tablespoons flour
1½ teaspoons butter
1 cup low-sodium chicken broth
3 teaspoons minced fresh ginger
3 teaspoons Dijon mustard
3 teaspoons grainy mustard
6 green onions, minced
Salt and pepper to taste

Dust chops lightly with flour.

Melt butter in a large skillet and sauté chops over medium heat until browned on both sides and cooked through, 3 to 5 minutes per side. Remove chops and keep warm.

Pour broth into skillet, increase heat, and deglaze skillet by boiling and scraping loose browned bits from bottom of pan. Add ginger and cook, stirring frequently, for 2 minutes. Stir in mustards and green onions. Season with salt and pepper.

Spoon sauce over chops and serve.

PER SERVING:
192 Calories; 8g Fat; 24g Protein; 5g Carbohydrate; 1g Dietary Fiber; 69mg Cholesterol; 216mg Sodium. Exchanges: 0 Grain (Starch); 3 Lean Meat; 0 Vegetable; 0 Fat; 0 Other Carbohydrates.

Serves 4–6

½ teaspoon chili powder

½ teaspoon garlic powder

½ teaspoon ground cumin

Salt and pepper to taste

4–6 (4–6 ounces each) turkey cutlets

2 tablespoons vegetable oil

1½ cups frozen corn kernels, thawed

½ cup salsa (your favorite)

3 tablespoons chopped fresh cilantro

1½ large tomatoes, chopped (about 1 cup)

1 (16-ounce) can black beans, rinsed and drained

Mix chili powder, garlic powder, cumin, salt, and pepper, then sprinkle evenly over both sides of turkey cutlets.

Heat oil in a large skillet over medium-high heat. Add turkey and sauté for 4 to 5 minutes per side, or until browned on both sides.

Add remaining ingredients. Heat to boiling, reduce heat, cover, and simmer for 3 to 5 minutes, or until turkey is no longer pink and vegetables are heated through. Serve.

PER SERVING:
237 Calories; 7g Fat ; 23g Protein; 22g Carbohydrate; 6g Dietary Fiber; 45mg Cholesterol; 495mg Sodium. Exchanges: 1 1/2 Grain (Starch); 2 1/2 Lean Meat; 1/2 Vegetable; 1 Fat.

FRENCH BEEF STEW

Serves 4–6

1 pound lean boneless beef, cut into 1-inch cubes

½ large onion, chopped

2 carrots, scraped and sliced diagonally into ¾-inch-thick ovals

1 small red bell pepper, de-ribbed, seeded, and cut into ½-inch strips

8 ounces small fresh mushrooms, cleaned

2 ripe tomatoes, cut into wedges

1 cup red wine (optional)

1 bay leaf

¼ cup chopped fresh parsley

1 teaspoon dried tarragon

½ teaspoon salt

¼ teaspoon black pepper

1 cup frozen peas, thawed (petite or baby are best)

In a slow-cooker, combine beef, onion, carrots, red bell pepper, mushrooms, tomatoes, wine, bay leaf, parsley, and tarragon. Cook on low for 5 to 6 hours, depending on your slow-cooker.

When the stew has cooked, stir in salt, black pepper, and peas; stir to mix and serve hot.

PER SERVING:
459 Calories; 14g Fat; 26g Protein; 52g Carbohydrate; 5g Dietary Fiber; 100mg Cholesterol; 295mg Sodium. Exchanges: 3 Grain (Starch); 2 Lean Meat; 1 1/2 Vegetable; 1 Fat.

TWO-STEP RECIPES

When you have a little more time, these two-step dinners will do the trick.

LEMON TARRAGON CHICKEN

1 tablespoon olive oil
Salt and pepper to taste
4–6 (4–6 ounces each) boneless skinless chicken breast halves
½ cup lemon juice
½ cup dry white wine or low-sodium chicken broth
¾ teaspoon dried tarragon
1½ tablespoons cornstarch
3 tablespoons water
1 lemon, thinly sliced

In a large skillet, heat oil 1 to 2 minutes over medium heat. Sprinkle salt and pepper over both sides of chicken. Cook chicken in hot skillet 5 to 6 minutes, turning once, until light brown. Remove the chicken from the skillet and set aside.

Add the lemon juice, wine or broth, and tarragon to the skillet. Scrape the browned bits from the bottom of the pan. Heat to boiling over high heat. Once mixture is boiling, return chicken to skillet and reduce heat just enough so mixture bubbles gently. Cover and cook 10 to 15 minutes, stirring occasionally, until chicken is cooked.

While the chicken is cooking, mix the cornstarch and water. When the chicken is done, remove from the skillet with a slotted spoon and keep warm. Stir cornstarch mixture into mixture in skillet. Cook over medium heat, stirring constantly, until mixture thickens and boils. Continue boiling 1 minute, stirring constantly. Pour sauce over chicken, garnish with lemon slices, and serve.

PER SERVING:
178 Calories; 4g Fat; 27g Protein; 5g Carbohydrate; trace Dietary Fiber; 68mg Cholesterol; 79mg Sodium. Exchanges: 0 Grain (Starch); 4 Lean Meat; 0 Fruit; 1/2 Fat.

Serves 4–6

NOTE: Feel free to
chop up any other
leftover veggies in your
crisper that you won't
use this week. Stir-fry is
perfect for this.

1½ tablespoons olive oil

1½ pounds skinless boneless chicken breasts, cut into 2-inch pieces

3 garlic cloves, pressed

2 bell peppers, de-ribbed, seeded, and cut into 1-inch pieces

1 large onion, thinly sliced

1 bunch broccoli, cut into little florets (see Note)

½ cup dry red wine or grape juice with a splash of vinegar

¾ teaspoon dried thyme

¾ teaspoon dried rosemary

Salt and pepper to taste

1½ tablespoons grated Parmesan cheese

Heat olive oil in 10-inch nonstick skillet or wok over medium-high heat. Add chicken and garlic; stir-fry until chicken is almost done, 3 to 4 minutes. Remove chicken from skillet or wok; keep warm.

Add remaining ingredients except cheese to skillet, then stir-fry until vegetables are crisp-tender, 3 to 4 minutes. Stir in chicken; heat until chicken is cooked through. Sprinkle with cheese and serve.

PER SERVING:
196 Calories; 5g Fat; 27g Protein; 5g Carbohydrate; 1g Dietary Fiber; 67mg Cholesterol; 112mg Sodium. Exchanges: 0 Grain (Starch); 3 1/2 Lean Meat; 1 Vegetable; 1/2 Fat.

POUNDED CHICKEN PARMESAN

Serves 4–6

1 cup grated Parmesan cheese
3 teaspoons dried oregano
1½ teaspoons paprika
Salt and pepper to taste
3 tablespoons butter
1½ tablespoons olive oil
4–6 boneless skinless chicken breast halves, flattened

Preheat oven to 350°F.

In a bowl, combine Parmesan, oregano, paprika, salt, and pepper. Line a shallow baking pan with foil.

In a skillet, melt butter and oil together. Dip each chicken breast in butter mixture, then cheese mixture and place in the foil-lined pan. Bake chicken for 30 minutes or until cooked through. Serve.

PER SERVING:
276 Calories; 15g Fat; 33g Protein; 1g Carbohydrate; trace Dietary Fiber; 94mg Cholesterol; 384mg Sodium. Exchanges: 0 Grain (Starch); 4 1/2 Lean Meat; 2 Fat.

CUBAN PORK

THIS DISH REQUIRES MARINATING THE NIGHT BEFORE.

Serves 6

½ cup orange juice
¼ cup lime juice
4 garlic cloves, pressed
2 tablespoons dried oregano
Salt and pepper to taste
2 pounds boneless pork loin

Combine first 5 ingredients for the marinade. Place pork in a dish and pour marinade over pork. Cover and refrigerate overnight.

The next day, preheat oven to 375°F. Place pork in a roasting pan, reserving marinade. Roast pork for about 45 minutes, or until it reaches an internal temperature of 165°F. Remove form oven and let rest 10 minutes before slicing.

While pork is resting, add reserved marinade to a small saucepan and bring to a boil, then simmer for a few minutes. Serve pork with herbed juices.

PER SERVING:
244 Calories; 14g Fat; 23g Protein; 5g Carbohydrate; 1g Dietary Fiber; 75mg Cholesterol; 68mg Sodium. Exchanges: 0 Grain (Starch); 3 Lean Meat; 0 Vegetable; 0 Fruit; 1 Fat.

GREEK SCAMPI PASTA

Serves 4–6

1 tablespoon olive oil
6 garlic cloves, pressed
2 (15-ounce) cans diced tomatoes (undrained)
½ cup chopped Italian parsley
2 pounds large shrimp, peeled and deveined
1 pound fettuccine, uncooked
1 cup crumbled feta cheese
2 tablespoons fresh lemon juice
Freshly ground pepper to taste

Preheat oven to 400°F. Put on a pot of water to boil for the pasta.

In a skillet over medium heat, heat oil. Add garlic and sauté 30 seconds, being careful not to brown. Add tomatoes and half the parsley. Reduce heat and simmer for about 10 minutes. Add the shrimp and cook 5 minutes.

Meanwhile, cook the pasta according to package directions.

Drain. Toss shrimp mixture with the hot pasta, and top with the feta cheese, remaining parsley, lemon juice, and pepper. Serve.

PER SERVING:
547 Calories; 11g Total Fat; 45g Protein; 64g Carbohydrate; 252mg Cholesterol; 617mg Sodium. Exchanges: 4 Grain (Starch); 5 Lean Meat; 1 Vegetable; 0 Fruit; 1 Fat; 0 Other Carbohydrates.

CREAMY MEXICAN COOKER PORK STEW

Serves 4–6

1½ tablespoons vegetable oil

1½ pounds boneless pork shoulder roast, cut into ¾-inch cubes

1 (14½-ounce) can low-sodium chicken broth

3–4 garlic cloves, pressed

½ cup sliced green onions

1 teaspoon dried oregano

1¼ cups salsa of choice

Salt and pepper

3 tablespoons flour

⅔ cup half-and-half

In a skillet, heat oil and brown pork over medium-high heat, about 6 to 8 minutes.

Stir in chicken broth, garlic, green onions, and oregano. Bring to a boil; add salsa, reduce heat, and simmer for 2 minutes, adding salt and pepper to taste. Transfer everything to a slow-cooker and cook on low for 8 hours.

Toward the end of cooking time, turn temperature to high. Combine flour and half-and-half, mixing until smooth. Gradually stir into stew. Keep the lid off and cook, stirring, until thickened. (Depending on the model and age of your slow-cooker, you may need to place stew in a pot to thicken on the stovetop.) It's not going to be too thick, but there is enough flour to tighten the sauce. If you prefer thicker sauce, stir in another tablespoon of flour. Serve.

PER SERVING:
358 Calories; 17g Fat; 23g Protein; 4g Carbohydrate; trace Dietary Fiber; 90mg Cholesterol; 523mg Sodium. Exchanges: 0 Grain (Starch); 3 Lean Meat; 0 Vegetable; 0 Nonfat Milk; 3 1/2 Fat.

BLUE CHEESE STEAKS

Serves 4–6

4–6 (6 ounces each) cube steaks, 1 inch thick
2 teaspoons garlic powder
Salt and pepper

CHEESE TOPPING

2 tablespoons cream cheese, softened
4 teaspoons crumbled blue cheese
4 teaspoons low-fat sour cream
2 teaspoons minced onion
Dash of white pepper

Preheat broiler. In small bowl, combine topping ingredients and set aside.

Sprinkle one side of the steaks with half the garlic powder, and salt and pepper to **taste**. Place the seasoned steaks on a rack of the broiler pan so that the meat is 2 to 3 inches from the heat source. Broil for 5 to 6 minutes. (Babysit your beef—don't walk away!)

Turn steaks and season with remaining garlic powder, salt, and pepper. Broil another 5 to 6 minutes.

Top each steak with an equal amount of cheese topping. Broil an additional 1 to 2 minutes to melt and *slightly* brown, if you like. Serve.

PER SERVING:
234 Calories; 16g Fat; 21g Protein; 1g Carbohydrate; trace Dietary Fiber; 71mg Cholesterol; 97mg Sodium. Exchanges: 3 Lean Meat; 0 Vegetable; 0 Nonfat Milk; 1 Fat; 0 Other Carbohydrates.

THREE-STEP RECIPES

Once you get your speed down a little (like the chopping and prepping portion of the recipe), you'll find that three-step dinners, such as these, will go fast and that the little extra work is so worth it. Here's a hint for paring down the steps: do some of these things in advance, like chopping the vegetables the night before; preparing dressings ahead; pre-cooking chicken, rice, or whatever else you might need for your recipe. And remember, a good cook reads through the recipe (not just checks the ingredients) to make sure he or she will know what to do and has the time to do it.

I learned this lesson when making chocolate pinwheel cookies as a middle schooler. After I was done making two types of dough, I noticed that I needed to refrigerate the dough. Well, the fact was I simply didn't have the time to refrigerate the dough—I was bringing these to school for party refreshments and had to go to bed. So after spending all that time making the vanilla and chocolate doughs, rolling them out separately, then putting them together, rolling them up into spiraled logs, cutting them in even little circles, and launching them into the oven, I watched in horror as my cookies grew to mammoth proportions, oozing off the cookie sheet and onto the bottom of the oven in a burning mess. Perhaps if I had read through the recipe, I would have (1) tried a less ambitious recipe on a school night and/or (2) planned a little better and chilled the dough. Let's just say that was a culinary lesson I learned well.

When my own daughter (at the time a middle schooler and wanting to bake cookies for a class) announced that she was baking something that required chilling before baking, I regaled her with this story, adding unnecessary and overly dramatic details to make my point. Unfortunately, my daughter chose the School of Hard Knocks way of doing things and she, too, saw her labor of love ooze to the bottom of the oven and stink up the house for three days. Thank heavens you can always buy themed cupcakes at the grocery store at 7 A.M., on your way to school.

Serves 4–6

6 ounces fine noodles

2 tablespoons olive oil

2 tablespoons white wine vinegar

3 tablespoons peanut butter

3 tablespoons soy sauce

1½ tablespoons honey

1½ teaspoons grated fresh ginger

¼ teaspoon red pepper flakes (optional)

1 teaspoon vegetable oil

2 teaspoons toasted sesame oil

1½ red or yellow bell peppers, de-ribbed, seeded, and cut into thin strips

6 green onions, bias-sliced into ½-inch lengths

4 (4–6 ounces each) boneless skinless chicken breast halves, cut into stir-fry strips

¼ cup coarsely chopped cashews

Cook noodles according to package directions. Drain and set aside.

In a blender, combine olive oil, vinegar, peanut butter, soy sauce, honey, ginger, and red pepper flakes. Blend until smooth.

In a large skillet, heat vegetable and sesame oils over medium-high heat. Add bell pepper strips and green onions; cook and stir for 1 to 2 minutes or until onions are crisp-tender. Remove vegetables from skillet.

Add chicken strips to hot skillet. Cook and stir for 2 to 3 minutes, or until cooked through.

Return vegetables to skillet and add cooked noodles. Cook and stir about 1 minute more or until heated through. Remove from heat.

Pour the dressing over mixture in skillet. Toss lightly to coat. Divide chicken mixture among individual plates. Sprinkle with cashews and serve.

PER SERVING:
393 Calories; 21g Fat; 21g Protein; 33g Carbohydrate; 3g Dietary Fiber; 54mg Cholesterol; 985mg Sodium. Exchanges: 1 1/2 Grain (Starch); 2 Lean Meat; 1 Vegetable; 2 1/2 Fat; 1/2 Other Carbohydrates.

WHITE CHICKEN LASAGNA ROLLS

Serves 4–6

18 uncooked manicotti (use jumbo pasta shells if you cannot find
  manicotti)

1½ tablespoons olive oil

1 (14.5-ounce) can diced tomatoes, drained

1 celery stalk, finely chopped

1½ carrots, finely chopped

3 garlic cloves, pressed

3 (4 ounces each) cooked chicken breast halves, diced

1½ tablespoons dry white wine or chicken broth

1½ (15-ounce) containers ricotta cheese

1½ cups seasoned croutons

1½ teaspoons chopped fresh parsley

Salt and pepper to taste

Cook pasta according to package directions; drain.

Preheat oven to 400°F. Grease an 8-inch-square baking pan.

In a skillet over medium-high heat, heat the oil. Cook tomatoes, celery, carrots, and garlic in oil 5 to 7 minutes, stirring frequently, until celery and carrots are crisp-tender. Stir in chicken and wine or broth. Cook 5 minutes, until wine or broth is evaporated.

Stir remaining ingredients into chicken mixture. Fill cooked shells with chicken mixture. Set in baking pan with filled-sides up. Bake uncovered about 10 minutes, or until filling is golden brown. Serve.

PER SERVING:
365 Calories; 14g Fat; 26g Protein; 31g Carbohydrate; 2g Dietary Fiber; 70mg Cholesterol; 171mg Sodium. Exchanges: 1 1/2 Grain (Starch); 3 Lean Meat; 1 Vegetable; 2 Fat.

GRILLED APRICOT-GLAZED PORK

Serves 4–6

1½ (10-ounce) jars apricot preserves
6 tablespoons orange juice
3 tablespoons butter
4–6 (4–6 ounces each) boneless pork chops, cut into 1-inch cubes
Skewers

Stir together apricot preserves, orange juice, and butter in a small saucepan and simmer until butter is melted. Let cool.

Place pork cubes in heavy plastic bag, pour ¾ cup apricot mixture over to coat, and marinate at least 30 minutes. Preheat a broiler or an outdoor grill.

Thread pork onto skewers (if using bamboo skewers, soak in water for 20 to 30 minutes before using). Grill over hot coals or in broiler 10 to 12 minutes, turning occasionally. Baste often with the marinade. Warm the remaining apricot marinade to boiling and serve alongside kabobs, if desired.

PER SERVING:
380 Calories; 12g Fat; 22g Protein; 47g Carbohydrate; 1g Dietary Fiber; 82mg Cholesterol; 139mg Sodium. Exchanges: 3 Lean Meat; 0 Fruit; 1 Fat; 3 Other Carbohydrates.

MY FABULOUS ROAST CHICKEN

Serves 4–6

1 roasting chicken (5–6 pounds), rinsed and patted dry
2 celery stalks, cut into 2-inch pieces
2 onions, quartered
2 carrots, cut into 2-inch pieces
Salt and pepper
Garlic powder
1 tablespoon flour
⅓ cup water

Preheat oven to 375°F. Rinse chicken and pat dry. Save the chicken neck.

Put 1 celery stalk, 1 onion, and 1 carrot inside the cavity of the bird; place chicken in a roasting pan and sprinkle with salt, pepper, and garlic powder to taste. Depending on the size of your bird, it should take about 1½ hours to roast. When the chicken is done, the leg will move easily in the socket.

While the chicken is cooking, place 1 carrot, 1 onion, 1 celery stalk, and the chicken neck in a 2-quart stockpot. Cover with water and cook on low for 30 to 45 minutes to make additional stock for the gravy. Set aside.

NOTE: Pick every last ever-lovin' bit of chicken off the bones for Part 2 of this recipe. Save the chicken carcass for Part 3 of this recipe.

MAKE THE GRAVY.

Remove bird from roaster and keep warm. Pour the cooking juices out of the roaster and into a bowl to cool. You can speed this process by putting the juice in the fridge or freezer; the fat will glob up on the top and then you can skim this nasty stuff off and throw it away. Return the de-fatted pan drippings to the roasting pan.

In a small mixing bowl, mix the flour and water into a smooth paste—no lumps allowed!

Heat the cooking juices, then add the neck stock and the flour-water paste. Using a wire whisk, whisk like a crazy woman over fairly high heat until your mixture starts to look like gravy. Remember, you want all those yummy browned bits on the bottom integrated into the gravy. That's what gives it its flavor. When nice and brown and beautiful, remove from heat; check for flavor and salt and pepper to taste, if necessary. Pour into a gravy boat. Carve chicken and serve with gravy.

PER SERVING:
364 Calories; 23g Fat; 30g Protein; 7g Carbohydrate; 2g Dietary Fiber; 141mg Cholesterol; 132mg Sodium. Exchanges: 0 Grain (Starch); 4 Lean Meat; 1 Vegetable; 2 Fat.

MY FABULOUS ROAST CHICKEN BURRITOS

Serves 4–6

> 2 cups chopped cooked chicken
> 1 (16-ounce) can black beans, drained and rinsed
> 1 teaspoon ground cumin
> 1 teaspoon garlic powder
> ½ cup jarred salsa, or more if desired
> 6 whole wheat flour tortillas
> Optional garnishes: shredded lettuce, shredded cheese, sour cream, chopped cilantro, avocado slices, chopped tomato

Mix chicken in a saucepan with beans, cumin, garlic powder, and salsa. Cook over medium-low heat to blend.

Warm tortillas by heating a dry skillet over medium heat for about 2 minutes. Add the tortillas one at a time, turning them with your fingers (just be careful not to touch the hot pan!). Place the warmed tortillas in a napkin-lined basket to keep warm till it's time to build your burritos. Fill tortillas with chicken-bean mixture and add garnishes of your choice. Serve.

PER SERVING:
363 Calories; 9g Fat; 18g Protein; 51g Carbohydrate; 6g Dietary Fiber; 27mg Cholesterol; 684mg Sodium. Exchanges: 3 1/2 Grain (Starch); 1 1/2 Lean Meat; 0 Vegetable; 1 Fat.

MY FABULOUS ROAST CHICKEN SOUP

Serves 4–6

1 small onion, chopped
1 tablespoon butter and a splash of olive oil
1 pound chopped veggies (carrots, celery, cabbage, turnips, zucchini,
  broccoli, etc.)
1 (14.5-ounce) can diced tomatoes
2 quarts chicken broth (page 86)
1 teaspoon garlic powder
1 teaspoon thyme
Salt and pepper to taste

In a soup pot, sauté the onion in butter and oil till almost clear, about 4 minutes.

Add the rest of the veggies and diced tomatoes. Sauté for a minute or two, then add the broth and seasonings. Simmer till the vegetables are tender. Serve.

PER SERVING:
117 Calories; 2g Fat; 10g Protein; 15g Carbohydrate; 4g Dietary Fiber; 0mg Cholesterol; 106mg Sodium. Exchanges: 0 Grain (Starch); 1/2 Lean Meat; 2 1/2 Vegetable; 0 Fat.

COMPANY POT ROAST

Serves 4–6

NOTE: This recipe allows for lots of leftovers to make barbecued beef sandwiches later in the week. Use leftovers within 4 days or freeze. Save any leftover gravy also.

3-pound beef roast, such as chuck roast
1 tablespoon olive oil
Salt and black pepper
½ cup water
6 garlic cloves, sliced

GRAVY
1½ tablespoons cornstarch
6 tablespoons water
Salt and pepper

Wash meat and pat dry. In a skillet, heat olive oil over medium-high heat. Season meat with salt and pepper to taste and brown on all sides. Place roast in slow-cooker, fat side down. Add the water to the skillet and turn up the heat. Using a wire whisk, get all the browned bits up off the bottom of the skillet to make a watery gravy. Pour this on top of the beef in the cooker.

Slice garlic into thin pieces and lay over the top. Sprinkle lightly with salt and pepper. Set dial on low and cook, covered, for about 5 hours. (Sometimes, relative to the density of the roast, it will be done in 4 hours. Check to see if the meat easily pulls apart when tested with a fork.)

Dissolve the cornstarch for the gravy in water; set aside. Pour cooker juices into a saucepan and heat on stovetop over medium heat. Whisk in the cornstarch mixture until sauce is nicely thickened. Salt and pepper to taste. Serve roast with gravy.

PER SERVING:
349 Calories; 12g Fat; 54g Protein; 4g Carbohydrate; trace Dietary Fiber; 134mg Cholesterol; 149mg Sodium. Exchanges: 0 Grain (Starch); 7 1/2 Lean Meat; 0 Vegetable; 0 Nonfat Milk; 0 Fat.

BARBECUE BEEF SANDWICHES

Serves 4–6

1½ *small onions, chopped*
2 *tablespoons vegetable oil*
4½ *cups shredded cooked pot roast*
Leftover gravy
9 *tablespoons barbecue sauce (your favorite)*
Salt and pepper
6 *hamburger buns*
18 *slices pickles (optional)*

In a large skillet, sauté onions in oil until brown and translucent, about 6 minutes.

Stir in beef and leftover gravy. Add barbecue sauce and simmer for about 10 minutes.

Add salt and pepper to taste. Spoon mixture onto hamburger buns and serve with pickle slices.

PER SERVING:
452 Calories; 17g Fat; 42g Protein; 30g Carbohydrate; 2g Dietary Fiber; 99mg Cholesterol; 605mg Sodium. Exchanges: 1 1/2 Grain (Starch); 5 1/2 Lean Meat; 1/2 Vegetable; 2 Fat; 1/2 Other Carbohydrates.

PORK PAILLARDS

4–6 (4–6 ounces each) boneless pork chops, about ½ inch thick
Salt and pepper to taste
4½ tablespoons olive oil
6 slices bacon
1 (12-ounce) bag fresh baby spinach
6 green onions, chopped
⅓ cup balsamic vinegar
3 tablespoons orange juice
⅓ cup golden raisins
3 tablespoons brown sugar
¾ cup blue cheese, crumbled

Season chops with salt and pepper. In a large skillet over medium-high heat, brown chops in 3 tablespoons oil until golden on each side, about 4 to 6 minutes.

Reduce heat to medium-low and continue to cook until chops are done, another 4 to 6 minutes. Remove from skillet and keep warm.

Add bacon to skillet and cook until crisp, about 8 minutes. Remove bacon from skillet and crumble. Reserve 2 teaspoons bacon drippings. Wipe out skillet.

Pour reserved bacon drippings back into skillet and sauté spinach for 2 to 3 minutes. Move spinach around so that all of the leaves are wilted. Once spinach is wilted, remove skillet from heat.

In a large saucepan, combine remaining 1½ tablespoons olive oil, green onions, balsamic vinegar, orange juice, raisins, and brown sugar; stir till sugar is dissolved.

Place pork chops on plates, top with wilted spinach, and drizzle on raisin dressing. Top with bacon bits and blue cheese, and serve.

PER SERVING:
388 Calories; 24g Fat; 29g Protein; 15g Carbohydrate; 2g Dietary Fiber; 83mg Cholesterol; 401mg Sodium. Exchanges: 3 1/2 Lean Meat; 1/2 Vegetable; 1/2 Fruit; 3 Fat; 1/2 Other Carbohydrates.

Crock-Pot Cornucopia
(From *Saving Dinner*. Ballantine, 2003)

All slow-cookers are *not* created equal. The following is a rule of thumb—your mileage may vary.

- Conventional Cooking Time: 15 to 30 minutes
  Slow-cooker Cooking Time: 1½ hours on high, 4 to 8 hours on low
- Conventional Cooking Time: 30 to 40 minutes
  Slow-cooker Cooking Time: 3 to 4 hours on high, 6 to 10 hours on low
- Conventional Cooking Time: 50 minutes to 3 hours
  Slow-cooker Cooking Time: 4 to 6 hours on high, 8 to 18 hours on low

Most stews, pot roasts, and other uncooked poultry or other meat and vegetable combinations require at least 4 to 6 hours on high, 8 hours on low.

CHAPTER ELEVEN

HOW TO BAKE
AND JUST DESSERTS

I t's no secret that I've avoided a lot of baking and dessert making. Desserts to me are an art form that I have not spent the time, energy, or calories on. Sure, I've done some cooking/baking, etc. in this sweet department, but considering that I've lost a substantial amount of weight and have happily landed in a pair of jeans boasting a single digit, I really need to watch my participation in this category of cooking. I know I would like it entirely too much and be sucked back into the sugar vortex that will leave my butt and thighs victimized and needing more fabric.

In the world of cooking, there are two types of people: them that cook food and them that bake sweets. In other words, bakers are different from the rest of us. They aspire to create perfect meringue while the rest of us rejoice in the creation of yet another skillet meal. We cook for pleasure, though sometimes it's for survival (this is when cooking isn't much fun). With bakers, it's all about hedonistic gratification.

Bakers are a subculture unto themselves. They are smitten with sweetness. When they made their first batch of Toll House cookies off the back of the chocolate chip bag, it wasn't just that they enjoyed the cookies, it was more of a religious experience.

Fortunately, there is always a reason to bend rules a little, and I've been known to bend one or two in my time. Take, for example, the holidays. Thanksgiving isn't complete without at least two different homemade pies. At Christmas, I bake on average five different cookies and make a decadent (but extremely easy) trifle for dessert (recipe in *Saving Dinner for the Holidays*). I find something fun to do with lemons and blueberries for Easter, and sometimes, I just bake for the heck of it. You don't always have to have a reason to make dessert, you know.

Like all good things in life, there are rules for baking that will help you get good results each time. I've included the ones that make a difference and some fabulous recipes after that. What else could you possibly want?

1. *Always start with reading your recipe*. How often have you been foiled by the need to refrigerate something (like cookie dough, etc.) before baking and just hadn't figured that time into the equation? And why did that happen? You know the answer—you didn't read through the recipe first. So that's where we always start: reading the recipe!

2. *Don't forget your* mise-en-place. This means you have all your tools and ingredients out and ready to roll. Remember we discussed this in a previous chapter? *Mise-en-place* when making dinner is important; it's critical when doing dessert.

3. *Make measuring meaningful*. Accurate measurements equal good results. If you're going to give baked goods a chance, you need to get acquainted with your wet and dry measurements and know how to use them correctly (see sidebar).

4. *Size matters*. At least when it comes to the correct baking pans. Trying to squeeze batter that belongs in a 10-inch pan into an 8-inch pan is a guaranteed mess in your oven, and it will give you way less than desirable results when it comes to the end product.

5. *Good ingredients at the right temperature*. Sorry, but I will never be a fan of margarine as a substitute for butter. Butter is better by far. And while we're talking about good ingredients, don't forget to make sure those good ingredients are the right temperature for baking. Often, eggs need to be room temperature for baking. Likewise,

butter "softened" doesn't mean liquefied in the microwave, although I've done that myself (and the results were less than adequate, truth be told).

Measuring Magic
(From *Saving Dinner*. Ballantine, 2003)

There are two types of measuring cups: dry and liquid measurements. The glass one is for liquid. Those cute little nesting measuring cups are for dry ingredients. Use the proper measuring cups for each ingredient—it makes a huge difference.

When you measure in glass, make sure you put your eyeball right there by the measurement. If you are standing up, looking down on the cup, your measurement will be way off.

When measuring dry ingredients, don't forget the old spoon-it-in-and-level-it-off routine. If you stick your dry measuring cup into a bag of flour, you will come out with more flour than you intended. The flour will pack down in the cup, making your measurement considerably more than you intended. So remember to spoon the flour (or other dry ingredient) into the dry measuring cup and use the back of a knife to level it off. The only dry ingredient that should be packed is brown sugar.

KANDI'S MOUNTAIN OF SIN ON A PLATE

Serves 12–18

Kandi Speegle is my assistant, and there are times when she has something fabulous to add to one of the Saving Dinner books—like Kitty Litter Cake, for example (in *Saving Dinner for the Holidays*). This time around, she decided to forgo the gross-out factor and show you how to sin so bad you'll need to go to confession after eating this dessert. This is a very rich cake. I know some people who can handle big slices of it and some who can handle only a little bitty sliver. This goes great with a cup of strong hot coffee to cut some of the sweetness.

> 1 (18.25-ounce) box German chocolate cake mix prepared according to package with water, vegetable oil, and eggs
> 1 (14-ounce) can sweetened condensed milk
> 1 (12.25-ounce) jar caramel topping sauce (not the quick-freeze type)
> ¾ (12-ounce) container frozen whipped topping (such as Cool Whip)
> ½ (8-ounce) bag toffee bits (Heath Bar–style)

Preheat oven to 350°F.

Prepare and bake cake in a glass 9 × 13-inch baking pan according to package directions. Cool cake completely, but do not remove it from baking pan.

When cake is completely cool, take a serving fork or the handle end of a wooden spoon and poke holes all over cake. Go to town on it, piercing it all over, but try not to destroy it. You want it aerated, not crumbled. Pour can of condensed milk over cake and allow to soak into cake. Let cake sit for a few minutes.

Next, pour jar of caramel sauce over cake. Allow caramel sauce to be absorbed. If caramel is puddling on top of cake, gently give cake a few more pokes with a fork.

Next, ice the top of cake with whipped topping. Sprinkle toffee bits over whipped topping and refrigerate until ready to serve.

PER SERVING:
334 Calories; 15g Fat; 4g Protein; 49g Carbohydrate; 1g Dietary Fiber; 45mg Cholesterol; 245mg Sodium. Exchanges: 0 Lean Meat; 3 Fat; 3 Other Carbohydrates.

GINGER MUFFINS

½ cup (1 stick) butter, softened
½ cup sugar
1 egg
1 cup molasses
3 cups all-purpose flour
1½ teaspoon baking soda
½ teaspoon salt
1 teaspoon ground ginger
1 teaspoon ground cinnamon
¼ teaspoon ground nutmeg
1 cup hot water
Ginger Muffin Glaze (recipe follows; optional)

Preheat oven to 375°F. Grease 12-cup muffin pan.

In a large bowl, cream together butter and sugar. Beat in egg, then molasses.

In a separate bowl, sift together flour, baking soda, salt, ginger, cinnamon, and nutmeg. Stir dry ingredients into molasses mixture. Slowly add hot water, beating until mixture is smooth.

Fill muffin cups two-thirds full. Bake for 20 to 25 minutes. Cool on a rack. Serve plain or glazed (see following recipe).

PER SERVING:
293 Calories; 8g Fat; 4g Protein; 51g Carbohydrate; 1g Dietary Fiber; 36mg Cholesterol; 340mg Sodium. Exchanges: 1 1/2 Grain (Starch); 0 Lean Meat; 1 1/2 Fat; 2 Other Carbohydrates.

GINGER MUFFIN GLAZE

Makes glaze for 12 muffins

3 tablespoons butter, softened
½ cup brown sugar
1 tablespoon honey
2 teaspoons warm water

Cream together butter and brown sugar. Slowly add honey and warm water, and beat till smooth and fluffy. Spread over ginger muffins as desired.

PER SERVING:
53 Calories; 3g Fat; trace Protein; 7g Carbohydrate; trace Dietary Fiber; 8mg Cholesterol; 32mg Sodium. Exchanges: 1/2 Fat; 1/2 Other Carbohydrates.

KIM'S HUMMINGBIRD CAKE

Serves 16

3 cups all-purpose flour
2 cups sugar
1 teaspoon baking soda
1 teaspoon salt
1½ teaspoons ground cinnamon
3 eggs, beaten
1 cup vegetable oil
1½ teaspoons vanilla extract
1 (8-ounce) can crushed pineapple, undrained
2 cups chopped pecans
2 cups chopped banana
Cream Cheese Frosting (recipe follows)

Preheat oven to 350°F. Grease three 9-inch-round cake pans.
Combine the first 5 ingredients in a large mixing bowl. Make a well (in other words, make a hole in the middle of the dry ingredients).

In a separate bowl, mix the eggs and oil; pour into well and stir into the dry mixture until dry ingredients are moistened. Do not beat. Stir in vanilla, pineapple with syrup, 1½ cups pecans, and bananas.

Spoon batter into cake pans. Bake for 25 to 30 minutes or until a wooden pick inserted in center comes out clean. Cool in pans on counter for 10 minutes. Remove from pans and cool completely.

Spread frosting (see following recipe) between layers and on top and sides of cake, then sprinkle with remaining ½ cup chopped pecans.

PER SERVING:
419 Calories; 22g Fat; 5g Protein; 54g Carbohydrate; 2g Dietary Fiber; 35mg Cholesterol; 224mg Sodium. Exchanges: 1 1/2 Grain (Starch); 0 Lean Meat; 1/2 Fruit; 4 Fat; 1 1/2 Other Carbohydrates.

CREAM CHEESE FROSTING

Makes enough to frost all 3 layers of Kim's Hummingbird Cake

1 (8-ounce) package cream cheese, softened
½ cup (1 stick) butter, softened
1 (16-ounce) package confectioners' sugar, sifted
1 teaspoon vanilla extract
½ cup finely chopped pecans

Combine cream cheese and butter in a large bowl, beating until smooth. Add sugar and vanilla; beat until light and fluffy. Add pecans to icing mixture and stir to incorporate.

PER SERVING:
234 Calories; 13g Fat; 1g Protein; 29g Carbohydrate; trace Dietary Fiber; 31mg Cholesterol; 101mg Sodium. Exchanges: 0 Grain (Starch); 0 Lean Meat; 2 1/2 Fat; 2 Other Carbohydrates.

BLUEBERRY CRUMBLE

Serves 9

3 cups blueberries, fresh or frozen
²⁄₃ cup granulated sugar
1 tablespoon lemon juice
½ cup rolled oats, old-fashioned or quick-cooking (not instant)
¼ cup all-purpose flour
¼ cup (½ stick) butter, cut into small pieces
¼ cup brown sugar
¼ teaspoon ground cinnamon

Preheat oven to 375°F. Lightly grease an 8-inch-square baking dish.

In a saucepan over medium heat, stir together berries and sugar. Stir constantly until berries become juicy and liquid has thickened. Stir in lemon juice. Remove from heat and pour berries into baking dish.

In a mixing bowl, combine remaining ingredients. Stir together until mixture is crumbly. Sprinkle dry mix over berries. Bake for 15 to 20 minutes, or until crumble is golden brown on top. Cool, then cut, serve, and enjoy.

PER SERVING:
175 Calories; 6g Fat; 1g Protein; 31g Carbohydrate; 2g Dietary Fiber; 14mg Cholesterol; 57mg Sodium. Exchanges: 1/2 Grain (Starch); 1/2 Fruit; 1 Fat; 1 Other Carbohydrates.

MOUNTAINOUS MACAROONS

Makes 12

I've spent the last 25 years of my life making these delicious cookies. To make them even better, melt a bag of chocolate chips in a double boiler (or just place a metal mixing bowl over a pan of boiling water) and dip the bottoms of the cooled cookies in the chocolate, then place them on a piece of parchment or waxed paper. When they have set, put on your seat belt because you're in for the cookie ride of your life. These are to die for!

> *⅓ cup all-purpose flour*
> *2½ cups shredded coconut*
> *Pinch of salt*
> *⅔ cup sweetened condensed milk*
> *1 teaspoon vanilla extract*

Preheat oven to 350°F. Grease a cookie sheet.

In a bowl, mix the flour, coconut, and salt.

In a separate bowl, stir together the condensed milk and vanilla.

Make a well in dry ingredients and fold wet ingredients into well. Stir to blend.

Make 12 big and high mountains on cookie sheet. Bake for 20 minutes. Cool for 5 minutes on cookie sheet, then finish cooling on rack.

PER SERVING:
125 Calories; 7g Fat; 2g Protein; 14g Carbohydrate; 2g Dietary Fiber; 6mg Cholesterol; 36mg Sodium. Exchanges: 0 Grain (Starch); 0 Fruit; 1 1/2 Fat; 1/2 Other Carbohydrates.

TRIPLE LAYER NO-BAKE CHEESECAKE

Serves 8

I think the triple-layer thing is a triple threat to mainland security, don't you? I mean, if we all ate triple anythings for very long, our thighs would need their own zip code. Go easy with this one unless you're establishing yourself as a new continent.

2½ cups fresh strawberries, halved
½ cup sugar
2½ tablespoons cornstarch
1 (8-ounce) package cream cheese, softened
1 (14-ounce) can sweetened condensed milk
⅓ cup lemon juice
1 teaspoon vanilla extract
1 (6-ounce) ready-made chocolate cookie crumb pie crust
1 ounce semisweet chocolate, melted (optional)

In a saucepan over medium heat, stir together strawberries, sugar, and cornstarch. Bring to a gentle boil. Remove from heat and let cool.

In a mixing bowl, beat cream cheese until fluffy. Gradually add condensed milk, stirring until smooth. Stir in lemon juice and vanilla.

Pour cream cheese mixture into crust. Top with strawberry sauce and chill at least 3 hours. Before serving, drizzle with chocolate, if desired.

PER SERVING:
460 Calories; 22g Fat; 8g Protein; 61g Carbohydrate; 2g Dietary Fiber; 48mg Cholesterol; 294mg Sodium. Exchanges: 0 Grain (Starch); 1/2 Lean Meat; 1/2 Fruit; 4 1/2 Fat; 3 1/2 Other Carbohydrates.

FAKE IT KEY LIME PIE

Serves 8

This recipe breaks a multitude of my own rules (like the whipped topping, for example), but my rationale is twofold: (1) it is totally easy and delicious; (2) it's one of those things that you don't do often, so it's okay. Maybe those are flimsy excuses and not anywhere close to a rationale, but I don't care, and you won't either once you taste this!

> *1 deep-dish graham cracker pie crust, baked*
> *1 (14-ounce) can sweetened condensed milk*
> *1 (6-ounce) container frozen limeade concentrate, thawed*
> *1 (12-ounce) container frozen whipped topping (like Cool Whip)*

Bake pie crust according to package directions. Let cool.

While pie crust is cooling, stir together condensed milk and limeade. Fold limeade mixture into whipped topping. Spoon into pie crust. Chill 1 hour. Keep your fingers out of the filling. Serve.

PER SERVING:
434 Calories; 21g Fat; 6g Protein; 57g Carbohydrate; 1g Dietary Fiber; 17mg Cholesterol; 220mg Sodium. Exchanges: 1/2 Grain (Starch); 0 Fruit; 4 Fat; 2 1/2 Other Carbohydrates.

MY MOM'S BANANA BREAD

Makes 1 loaf or 2 mini loaves

Nothing exotic here—just a good reason to use up those very ripe bananas! I like warm banana bread with a glass of cold milk on a chilly winter afternoon. You'll love the nutty cinnamon-y crust—yum!

1 cup brown sugar
½ cup (1 stick) butter, softened
2 eggs, beaten
2 bananas, mashed
¼ cup buttermilk
2 cups all-purpose flour
½ teaspoon salt
1 teaspoon baking soda
½ cup chopped pecans
¼ cup granulated sugar
1 teaspoon ground cinnamon

Preheat oven to 350°F. Lightly grease a 9-inch loaf pan.

In a large mixing bowl, cream brown sugar and butter. Add eggs and bananas and blend well. Add buttermilk and stir again.

In a separate bowl, sift together flour, salt, and baking soda. Add dry ingredients to wet ingredients and blend well.

Stir pecans into batter and pour into loaf pan. Bake for 45 minutes to 1 hour.

While banana bread is baking, prepare cinnamon-sugar topping by mixing cinnamon and granulated sugar. (You may already have this mixture on your pantry shelf for cinnamon toast.) Remove banana bread from oven and sprinkle with cinnamon sugar while still warm. Let cool for at least 15 minutes before slicing.

PER SERVING:
259 Calories; 12g Fat; 4g Protein; 36g Carbohydrate; 3g Dietary Fiber; 52mg Cholesterol; 292mg Sodium. Exchanges: 1 Grain (Starch); 0 Lean Meat; 1/2 Fruit; 0 Nonfat Milk; 2 1/2 Fat; 1 Other Carbohydrates.

DING BATS

A great snack for kids. If you can get brown rice cereal and forgo the confectioners' sugar, you can almost enjoy these guilt-free.

¾ cup (1½ sticks) butter
½ cup honey
1 (8-ounce) package pitted dates, finely chopped
¾ cup water
2 cups puffed rice cereal
1 cup chopped pecans
Confectioners' sugar

In a large saucepan over low heat, melt butter. Stir in honey, dates, and water and stir until mixture is thickened. Watch it like a hawk, as you don't want this to scorch. Take off the heat and continue to stir until dates are totally melted.

Quickly add puffed rice cereal and nuts to saucepan. Stir gently to coat nuts. After a moment or so, the mixture should be cooled enough. Use your hands to roll into golf ball blobs. Roll balls in confectioners' sugar and place on parchment paper to cool. Store or eat immediately.

PER SERVING:
201 Calories; 12g Fat; 1g Protein; 25g Carbohydrate; 1g Dietary Fiber; 21mg Cholesterol; 79mg Sodium. Exchanges: 0 Grain (Starch); 0 Lean Meat; 1/2 Fruit; 2 1/2 Fat; 1 Other Carbohydrates.

OUTSIDE-IN FROSTING CAKE

Serves 12

1 (18.25-ounce) yellow cake mix
4 eggs
⅔ cup vegetable oil
1⅓ cups water
1 (16-ounce) can coconut pecan frosting
½ cup chopped pecans

Preheat oven to 350°F. Grease a 10-inch Bundt or tube cake pan.

In a mixing bowl, blend together cake mix, eggs, oil, and water until well incorporated. Add frosting to cake mix and mix well. Next add pecans and stir again until well blended.

Pour batter into cake pan and bake for 45 to 60 minutes, or until a cake tester inserted in the middle comes out clean. Remove pan from oven and invert over serving platter. This allows cake to be removed from pan while it is still warm. Allow cake to cool on serving platter. Slice and serve.

PER SERVING:
500 Calories; 31g Fat; 5g Protein; 55g Carbohydrate; 1g Dietary Fiber; 63mg Cholesterol; 376mg Sodium. Exchanges: 0 Grain (Starch); 1/2 Lean Meat; 6 Fat; 3 1/2 Other Carbohydrates.

LINZER BARS

I love Linzer tarts from a good bakery. These are almost as good and a lot faster to make!

> 1 cup all-purpose flour
> ½ cup honey
> 1 cup ground walnuts
> ½ cup (1 stick) butter, softened
> ½ teaspoon ground cinnamon
> ⅔ cup all-natural no-sugar-added raspberry preserves

Preheat oven to 375°F.

Mix all ingredients except preserves in a large bowl until crumbly.

Press two-thirds of crumb mixture into 9-inch-square baking pan. Spread crumb crust with preserves. Sprinkle remaining crumb mixture on top of preserves.

Bake for 20 to 25 minutes or until golden brown. Cool completely before cutting into squares. Measure squares by cutting bars into 8 rows by 6 rows.

PER SERVING:
58 Calories; 3g Fat; 1g Protein; 8g Carbohydrate; trace Dietary Fiber; 5mg Cholesterol; 21mg Sodium. Exchanges: 0 Grain (Starch); 0 Lean Meat; 1/2 Fat; 1/2 Other Carbohydrates.

BERRY KUCHEN

1 cup all-purpose flour
¼ teaspoon salt
⅛ teaspoon baking powder
¼ cup (½ stick) butter, softened
1 tablespoon honey
1½ cups fresh or frozen berries
¼ cup honey
1 teaspoon ground cinnamon
2 egg yolks
1 cup whipping cream

Preheat oven to 400°F.

Sift together flour, salt, and baking powder. Work in butter and honey until mixture is crumbly.

Pat mixture firmly and evenly in bottom and halfway up sides of an 8-inch-square baking dish. Arrange berries in pan.

Mix honey and cinnamon and drizzle over fruit. Bake for 15 minutes.

While kuchen is baking, blend together egg yolks and cream. Pour over fruit and bake another 25 minutes, or until custard is set and edges are lightly browned. Serve warm.

PER SERVING:
237 Calories; 16g Fat; 3g Protein; 21g Carbohydrate; 1g Dietary Fiber; 97mg Cholesterol; 130mg Sodium. Exchanges: 1/2 Grain (Starch); 0 Lean Meat; 0 Nonfat Milk; 3 Fat; 1/2 Other Carbohydrates.

WICKEDLY CHOCOLATE CAKE

This is an excellent cake to give and to get. Easy to make, easier to eat!

> *2 cups all-purpose flour*
> *1 cup sugar*
> *¼ cup unsweetened cocoa powder*
> *2 teaspoons salt*
> *1 teaspoon baking powder*
> *2 eggs*
> *¼ cup (½ stick) butter, melted*
> *1 cup buttermilk*
> *1 teaspoon vanilla extract*
> *½ cup chocolate chips*

Preheat oven to 350°F. Grease 9 × 13-inch baking pan.

In a large bowl, mix flour, sugar, cocoa, salt, and baking powder and make a well in the center.

In a medium bowl, beat together eggs, butter, buttermilk, and vanilla. Incorporate wet ingredients into dry and stir well.

Pour batter into baking pan and sprinkle with chocolate chips. Bake for 20 to 30 minutes, or until toothpick inserted in middle comes out clean. Remove from oven, cool for 20 minutes before slicing.

PER SERVING:
234 Calories; 8g Fat; 5g Protein; 39g Carbohydrate; 4g Dietary Fiber; 42mg Cholesterol; 469mg Sodium. Exchanges: 1 Grain (Starch); 0 Lean Meat; 0 Nonfat Milk; 1 1/2 Fat; 1 1/2 Other Carbohydrates.

INDEX

Leanne Ely is considered *the* expert on family cooking and healthy eating. She is a syndicated newspaper columnist (The Dinner Diva), a certified nutritionist, and the host of SavingDinner.com. Ely has a weekly "Food for Thought" column on the ever-popular FlyLady.net website, as well as her own e-zine, Healthy Foods. She is the author of *Saving Dinner, Saving Dinner the Low-Carb Way*, and *Saving Dinner for the Holidays*. She lives in North Carolina with her two teenage children.